ANDROID APP DEVELOPMENT FOR BEGINNERS

Learn Android Studio, Java, and Kotlin to Build Your First App

THOMPSON CARTER

Table of Contents

INTRODUCTION

"Android App Development for Beginners"

In the last decade, mobile applications have become an integral part of everyday life. From checking emails to ordering food, communicating with loved ones, managing finances, or even learning new languages, mobile apps cover every aspect of our daily routines. Android, Google's mobile operating system, powers billions of devices worldwide, making it one of the most popular platforms for mobile app development. Whether you're a budding developer with no prior experience or a seasoned programmer looking to branch into mobile development, this book, "Android App Development for Beginners," is crafted to be your complete guide to building practical, user-friendly Android applications.

Why Android?

Android is not only the most widely used mobile operating system, but it also has an open-source nature, a robust developer community, and a vast ecosystem of libraries, tools, and resources. Android's versatility allows developers to target a wide variety of devices, from high-end smartphones and tablets to wearables, TVs, and even IoT devices. Learning to develop for Android opens doors to creating diverse applications that reach users across the globe.

Additionally, Android provides developers with extensive resources through libraries, official tools, and documentation, which significantly eases the learning curve. With Android Studio, the official integrated development environment (IDE) for Android, and Kotlin, the preferred programming language for Android development, Google has created an ecosystem that prioritizes ease of use, efficiency, and developer productivity. This book will guide you through setting up this powerful environment and gradually introduce the skills necessary to build fully functional Android apps.

Who Is This Book For?

This book is intended for anyone interested in Android development, particularly beginners. It doesn't assume prior knowledge of Android or mobile development, but familiarity with programming fundamentals, especially object-oriented programming, will be helpful. Each chapter is carefully designed to introduce core concepts in a structured, approachable way. Alongside coding exercises and practical examples, we'll provide context for why each concept matters and how it fits into real-world application development.

Whether you're a student, a professional looking to switch careers, or a self-taught programmer, this book is structured to be your step-by-step guide from understanding the basics to developing full-fledged Android applications. By the end, you will not only know how to code but also understand the intricacies of app design, user interaction, performance optimization, and app publishing.

How This Book is Structured

The book is divided into 22 chapters, each focusing on a specific area of Android development. Starting from the basics, each chapter builds on the last, introducing new topics with practical code examples, visual aids, and exercises. You'll start by setting up your environment, learning about Android Studio and Kotlin, and gradually progress through the fundamentals of UI design, data storage, networking, background processing, and more. The later chapters delve into advanced topics like Firebase integration, handling animations, and optimizing app performance.

Each chapter includes:

- **Concept Introductions**: An overview of the topic, explaining its relevance and how it integrates with other aspects of Android development.
- **Code Examples**: Practical, jargon-free code snippets to demonstrate real-world applications of each concept.
- **Exercises**: Hands-on exercises to reinforce learning, with guided instructions for implementing solutions.
- **Real-World Examples**: Every chapter includes examples of how the concepts are applied in real-world applications, allowing you to see how your learning can be put into practice.

Here's a quick look at what you'll cover in the book:

- **Chapters 1-5**: These chapters introduce Android, the setup of Android Studio, and the basics of the Kotlin programming language. You'll learn about core Android components and understand how to structure and launch an Android app.
- **Chapters 6-10**: These chapters guide you through building intuitive user interfaces with XML, creating responsive layouts, and managing UI interactions. You'll understand how to use Android's core layout components like ConstraintLayout, Views, and Fragments to create effective UI designs.
- **Chapters 11-14**: Focusing on data and media, these chapters introduce data storage options, such as SharedPreferences, SQLite, and RecyclerView for displaying lists. You'll also explore handling multimedia like images, audio, and video to enhance user engagement.
- **Chapters 15-18**: These chapters cover more advanced topics like location services, Google Maps integration, working with animations, and managing permissions. These features allow you to add location-based features, design smooth transitions, and handle permissions safely.
- **Chapters 19-21**: Firebase integration, app testing, debugging, and optimization. Here, you'll learn to implement authentication, data storage with Firebase, and debug and optimize your apps for performance.

- **Chapter 22**: The final chapter provides a comprehensive guide to publishing your app on the Google Play Store, from setting up a developer account and preparing your app for release to creating a compelling app listing and promoting your app.

Learning Through Practical Application

Each concept in this book is introduced with real-world context. For instance, when you learn about data storage, you'll implement a note-taking app, complete with saving, updating, and deleting notes. When covering RecyclerView, we'll build a contact list app. By the time you reach advanced topics like Firebase and location-based services, you'll have already built a portfolio of apps that combine multiple Android features, giving you the confidence to bring your ideas to life.

We take a hands-on approach, ensuring you actively code along with each topic. The goal is for you to feel comfortable building your own applications and addressing real challenges faced by Android developers. This approach enables you to develop the skills necessary to build user-centric, polished, and reliable Android applications.

Preparing for Your Android Development Journey

Android development is an exciting, rapidly evolving field that provides endless opportunities for creativity and innovation. While the learning curve can be steep, this book's progressive structure, real-world examples, and hands-on exercises are designed to make your journey as smooth as possible. By the end of the book, you will be able to:

1. **Build Android Apps from Scratch**: From simple "Hello World" projects to more complex applications, you'll know how to create apps tailored to meet specific user needs.
2. **Implement Core Android Features**: Master essential Android components, such as activities, fragments, intents, notifications, data storage, location services, and more.
3. **Optimize Apps for Performance and User Experience**: Learn how to make your app responsive, visually appealing, and efficient in terms of memory and power usage.
4. **Prepare and Publish Your App**: Gain insights into the process of publishing an app on the Google Play Store and understand how to maintain and promote your app post-launch.

Why This Book is Unique

"Android App Development for Beginners" is unique because it takes a beginner-friendly, comprehensive approach to the entire Android development lifecycle. By combining theory with practical application, this book prepares you to build apps that are not only functional but also polished and optimized for a great user experience.

This book emphasizes learning without the typical jargon, making it accessible to everyone, regardless of technical background. Furthermore, each chapter is a stepping-stone that brings you closer to realizing your own app ideas, with practical guidance on overcoming common hurdles and optimizing your app's performance. By the end, you'll be equipped not only with technical skills but also with a problem-solving mindset essential for mobile development.

A Future-Ready Skill Set

The mobile development industry is constantly evolving. By learning Android app development, you're investing in a future-proof skill that's in high demand. Whether you're interested in freelancing, launching your own apps, or joining a development team, this book will equip you with the foundation and confidence to pursue these opportunities. Android development continues to expand into areas like IoT, wearables, and virtual reality, so the skills you learn here will be applicable across a broad spectrum of future technologies.

The journey to becoming an Android developer is rewarding and filled with opportunities for growth and creativity. This book is designed to support you at every step, from understanding Android basics to mastering app optimization and preparing for launch. With each chapter, you'll gain new insights and skills that will help you transition from a beginner to a confident Android developer.

Welcome to "Android App Development for Beginners"—let's start building!

CHAPTER 1: INTRODUCTION TO ANDROID DEVELOPMENT

In this first chapter, we'll introduce you to the Android platform, provide an overview of the goals and structure of this book, and look at some real-world examples of successful Android applications. By the end of this chapter, you should have a solid understanding of Android's ecosystem and why learning to develop Android apps can open up exciting opportunities.

Overview of Android as a Platform

What is Android?

Android is a mobile operating system developed by Google and designed primarily for touchscreen devices like smartphones and tablets. It is based on a modified version of the Linux kernel and other open-source software, which makes it customizable, versatile, and accessible to developers worldwide.

Android's architecture allows it to manage a range of hardware and software resources efficiently, from touch inputs and sensors to data storage and connectivity. This robust foundation is what enables Android to run smoothly on diverse devices, from low-cost smartphones to high-end tablets and even wearable tech.

The Android Ecosystem

The Android ecosystem encompasses more than just the operating system itself. It includes:

- **Google Play Store**: The primary marketplace where developers can publish apps and users can download them.
- **Google Mobile Services (GMS)**: A suite of services provided by Google, such as Google Maps, Google Search, Google Drive, and Google Play, that enhance the functionality and experience of Android apps.
- **Android Developer Community**: A vast community of developers, designers, and companies that collaborate, share resources, and continuously improve the platform.
- **Android Hardware Variety**: Android powers a range of devices beyond smartphones, including tablets, wearables (smartwatches), TVs, cars, and Internet of Things (IoT) devices.

Why Android is Popular

Android is the most widely used mobile operating system globally, with billions of active devices. Several factors contribute to Android's popularity:

- **Open Source and Customizability**: Android is an open-source platform, which means it's freely available for anyone to use, modify, and distribute. This has made Android popular among manufacturers who can tailor the OS to suit their hardware.

- **Wide Device Compatibility**: Android runs on a diverse range of devices across different price points, making it accessible to people worldwide.
- **Google's Support and Resources**: Google provides extensive support for Android development, including a vast array of libraries, development tools, and resources that make it easier to build powerful apps.
- **Vast Market Reach**: Since Android is the dominant mobile OS in many regions, developing for Android gives you access to a large potential audience, whether you're building a personal project or a business app.

Setting Up Goals for This Book

This book is designed to guide you from a complete beginner to a confident Android developer who can build and publish functional, real-world applications. We'll break down complex concepts and avoid technical jargon wherever possible, focusing on hands-on experience with practical examples.

What You Can Expect to Learn:

1. **Foundational Concepts**: We'll start with the basics of Android, including setting up your development environment, understanding Android Studio, and learning Kotlin (the primary programming language for Android development).

2. **Core Android Components**: You'll learn about the essential building blocks of an Android app, including activities, fragments, services, and content providers.
3. **User Interface Design**: We'll cover how to design responsive, user-friendly interfaces with XML layouts and various UI components.
4. **Data Management**: You'll understand how to store and retrieve data using options like SharedPreferences, SQLite databases, and cloud storage with Firebase.
5. **Networking**: We'll look at how to connect your app to the internet, retrieve data from APIs, and use libraries like Retrofit for efficient networking.
6. **Advanced Features**: As you progress, we'll introduce features like notifications, animations, multimedia, location services, and handling permissions.
7. **Testing, Optimization, and Publishing**: Finally, we'll guide you through testing, debugging, optimizing performance, and publishing your app on the Google Play Store.

This step-by-step progression ensures that by the end of this book, you'll have a thorough understanding of how to develop Android apps from start to finish.

Real-World Examples of Android Apps

To inspire you and show you what's possible with Android, let's look at some popular apps built on the platform. These examples highlight the wide range of possibilities with Android development.

1. WhatsApp

WhatsApp is one of the most popular messaging apps globally, known for its simplicity, reliability, and security. It allows users to send text messages, voice messages, images, videos, and documents. WhatsApp's success lies in its efficient use of Android's networking and messaging components, real-time notifications, and user-friendly interface.

2. Google Maps

Google Maps provides navigation, live traffic updates, local business information, and location sharing. It utilizes a wide array of Android features, including location services, real-time data processing, and API integration for retrieving location-based data. The app's offline mode and detailed map rendering showcase Android's capability to handle complex data and provide a seamless user experience.

3. Instagram

Instagram is a widely used photo and video-sharing social media app. Its functionality includes uploading photos, applying filters, liking and commenting on posts, and sharing stories. Instagram's success on Android is attributed to its ability to handle multimedia, integrate with the camera, display high-quality visuals, and utilize push notifications to keep users engaged.

4. Spotify

Spotify is a music streaming app that provides access to millions of songs, podcasts, and playlists. It utilizes various Android components, such as background services for music playback, media player controls, and complex networking for data streaming. The app is optimized to deliver a smooth, high-quality listening experience across different Android devices.

5. Uber

Uber is a ride-hailing app that connects riders with drivers. It relies on location services, real-time data synchronization, secure payment integration, and map-based navigation. Uber demonstrates the versatility of Android's APIs for handling multiple tasks at once, ensuring users can seamlessly book and track rides in real-time.

6. Duolingo

Duolingo is an educational app that helps users learn new languages through gamified lessons. The app's interactive design makes extensive use of animations, notifications, and in-app rewards to engage learners. Duolingo showcases how Android's animation and user interface components can be used to create an interactive and rewarding learning experience.

Why You Should Learn Android Development

These real-world examples show that Android development offers the flexibility and tools needed to create innovative applications. The Android ecosystem enables developers to reach billions of users across the globe, from communication and navigation to entertainment and education.

By learning Android development, you can:

- **Express Your Creativity**: Build unique apps that solve problems, entertain, educate, or enhance users' lives.
- **Enter a Lucrative Job Market**: Android developers are in high demand across various industries.
- **Reach a Global Audience**: Publishing on the Google Play Store allows you to make your app available to users worldwide.
- **Adapt to New Technologies**: Android development is continually evolving, allowing you to work with cutting-edge technologies like augmented reality, machine learning, and IoT.

What to Expect Moving Forward

As we move through this book, you'll gain hands-on experience building Android apps from the ground up. Each chapter is crafted to give you the skills you need to develop functional, engaging, and reliable Android applications.

The journey begins with setting up your development environment and understanding the Android Studio workspace. Then, you'll move through foundational concepts, learn the core components of Android development, and build several hands-on projects. Finally, you'll polish, test, and publish your app, creating a project that you can proudly showcase on the Google Play Store or use as a springboard to more advanced development.

With each chapter, you'll become more confident in your abilities, learning not only how to code but also how to think like an Android developer. By the end of this book, you'll have the knowledge and skills to bring your ideas to life on the world's most popular mobile operating system.

CHAPTER 2: SETTING UP YOUR DEVELOPMENT ENVIRONMENT

Setting up your development environment is the first step toward becoming an Android developer. In this chapter, we'll walk you through installing Android Studio, setting up the Android SDK and emulator, and creating your first project. By the end of this chapter, you'll have everything you need to start building Android apps.

Installing Android Studio: Step-by-Step Guide

Android Studio is the official integrated development environment (IDE) for Android development, created by Google. It includes everything you need to build Android apps, from a powerful code editor to a suite of tools for testing and debugging.

Step 1: Downloading Android Studio

1. Go to the official Android Studio download page.
2. Click the download button, and make sure to select the version compatible with your operating system (Windows, macOS, or Linux).
3. Accept the terms and conditions, then download the installer file.

Step 2: Installing Android Studio

1. **Windows**: Run the downloaded .exe file and follow the installation wizard. You'll have the option to choose an installation location.
2. **macOS**: Open the downloaded .dmg file and drag Android Studio to your Applications folder.
3. **Linux**: Extract the downloaded .zip file to a directory of your choice, then run the studio.sh file located in the android-studio/bin folder.

Step 3: Setting Up Android Studio

1. Open Android Studio once the installation is complete. You'll be prompted to download additional components, including the Android SDK.
2. Choose the **Standard** setup option to install essential tools and recommended settings.
3. During setup, you may be asked to specify the location for the Android SDK. Use the default location unless you have specific requirements.

Step 4: Verifying Installation

After installation, open Android Studio and wait for it to load. You'll see the Android Studio welcome screen, which means your installation is successful and you're ready to start creating projects.

Understanding Android SDK and Emulator

What is the Android SDK?

The **Android Software Development Kit (SDK)** is a collection of tools, libraries, and documentation that developers need to create Android apps. The SDK includes:

- **Build Tools**: Tools for compiling and packaging apps.
- **Android Libraries**: Libraries that provide essential Android functionality.
- **Documentation and Sample Code**: Guides and examples to help you understand how Android works.

The SDK is updated regularly, so Android Studio includes a tool called the **SDK Manager** to help you download and update specific components.

Using the SDK Manager

1. To open the SDK Manager, go to **Tools > SDK Manager** in Android Studio.
2. In the SDK Manager, you'll see a list of available SDK components, including **SDK Platforms** (different Android versions) and **SDK Tools** (tools for development and testing).

3. Select the latest SDK Platform (or other versions if needed) and install them to ensure compatibility with the latest Android features.

Setting Up an Android Emulator

The Android Emulator is a virtual device that lets you test your apps on various screen sizes, resolutions, and Android versions without needing a physical device.

Creating a Virtual Device:

1. Open the **AVD (Android Virtual Device) Manager** by going to **Tools > AVD Manager**.
2. Click **Create Virtual Device**. You'll see a list of available devices, such as Pixel phones and tablets.
3. Choose a device configuration that suits your needs (e.g., Pixel 4) and click **Next**.
4. Select the Android version for the emulator. If necessary, download the selected version by clicking **Download** next to the system image.
5. Once downloaded, click **Next**, then **Finish** to create your virtual device.

Running the Emulator:

1. In the AVD Manager, you'll see your newly created virtual device. Click the **Play** icon next to it to start the emulator.

2. The emulator will take a moment to load. Once it's running, it acts like a real Android device, allowing you to test your app's features and user interface.

Tip: You can use the emulator to test various configurations (such as screen orientation and battery levels) to ensure your app works across different device scenarios.

Setting Up Your First Project: Creating a "Hello World" App

Now that you have Android Studio and the emulator set up, it's time to create your first Android app. This simple "Hello World" app will help you get familiar with the development environment and understand how Android projects are structured.

Step 1: Creating a New Project

1. From the Android Studio welcome screen, click **Start a new Android Studio project**.
2. Choose a template for your project. For this example, select the **Empty Activity** template, which provides a blank screen with minimal code.
3. Click **Next** to proceed to the project configuration screen.

Step 2: Configuring Your Project

1. **Name**: Enter a name for your project (e.g., "HelloWorld").

2. **Package Name**: This is a unique identifier for your app. You can use the default package name that Android Studio suggests (e.g., com.example.helloworld).
3. **Save Location**: Choose a location on your computer where you want to save the project files.
4. **Language**: Select **Kotlin** as the programming language for the project.
5. **Minimum API Level**: This setting determines the minimum Android version that can run your app. Choose **API 21: Android 5.0 (Lollipop)** to support a wide range of devices.

Click **Finish** to create your project. Android Studio will create a new project folder with all the necessary files.

Step 3: Understanding the Project Structure

Once your project is created, Android Studio will open the main editor window, showing a structured view of your project. Here's an overview of the important folders and files:

- **Java/Kotlin Folder**: Contains your app's source code. Inside this folder, you'll find the MainActivity.kt file, which is the entry point of your app.
- **res (Resources) Folder**: Contains resources like layouts, images, and strings. The **layout** subfolder contains

activity_main.xml, where you define your app's user interface.

- **AndroidManifest.xml**: A configuration file that defines the essential information about your app, such as its package name, components, and permissions.

Step 4: Editing the Layout (activity_main.xml)

Let's customize the app to display "Hello, World!" on the screen.

1. In the **Project** pane, navigate to **res** > **layout** and open activity_main.xml.
2. You'll see a visual editor where you can design the layout. In this example, we'll use a TextView element to display the text.
3. In the activity_main.xml file, make sure the code includes a TextView with the text "Hello, World!".

```
xml
<?xml version="1.0" encoding="utf-8"?>
<RelativeLayout
xmlns:android="http://schemas.android.com/apk/res/android"
    android:layout_width="match_parent"
    android:layout_height="match_parent">

    <TextView
        android:layout_width="wrap_content"
```

```
    android:layout_height="wrap_content"
    android:text="Hello, World!"
    android:layout_centerInParent="true"
    android:textSize="24sp" />

</RelativeLayout>
```

This code places a TextView in the center of the screen and sets its text to "Hello, World!".

Step 5: Running the App on the Emulator

1. Once you've edited the layout, click the **Run** button (the green triangle) at the top of Android Studio.
2. Choose your virtual device from the list of available devices and click **OK** to start the app.
3. The app will build and launch on the emulator, displaying "Hello, World!" in the center of the screen.

If everything went well, congratulations—you've just created and launched your first Android app!

In this chapter, you successfully set up your development environment by installing Android Studio, configuring the Android SDK, and creating a virtual device with the emulator. You created your first project, "Hello World," which introduced you to the basic project structure and how to display text on the screen.

With this foundational setup, you're ready to dive into the core concepts of Android development. In the next chapter, we'll explore the basics of Android Studio, so you can become comfortable navigating the IDE and using its features to develop your app efficiently.

Chapter 3: Understanding the Basics of Android Studio

Android Studio is a powerful and comprehensive tool that provides everything you need to develop Android applications. In this chapter, we'll dive into Android Studio's core features, show you how to create and manage projects, and introduce debugging basics. By the end of this chapter, you'll be comfortable navigating the IDE and equipped with essential tools for efficient app development.

Exploring the IDE: Overview of Android Studio's Main Features and Panels

Android Studio offers a variety of features and panels that streamline Android development. Let's explore some of the most important components of the IDE.

1. Project Pane

The **Project Pane** (on the left side of the screen) shows the structure of your project files and directories. It organizes files into folders for Java/Kotlin code, resources (such as images and layouts), and configuration files.

- **Android View**: This is the default view in the Project Pane, organizing files into logical categories like java, res, and manifests. This view helps simplify navigation by grouping related files.

- **Project View**: Shows the physical file structure on your system. This is helpful when you need direct access to files as they appear in your file system.

2. Code Editor

The **Code Editor** is the main area where you write and edit your app's code. Key features include:

- **Syntax Highlighting**: Colors different parts of your code to improve readability.
- **Auto-Complete**: Suggests code completions and methods as you type, speeding up development.
- **Error Highlighting**: Identifies syntax errors and potential issues as you write, making it easier to spot and correct mistakes.

3. Layout Editor

The **Layout Editor** is a graphical editor for designing the UI of your app. It allows you to drag and drop UI components, such as TextView, Button, and ImageView, onto the screen, making it easier to visualize the layout.

- **Design Mode**: Lets you visually arrange UI components.
- **Code Mode**: Displays the XML code for the layout, where you can make manual adjustments.

- **Split Mode**: Shows both the design and XML code side-by-side, allowing you to edit either view while seeing changes reflected in real-time.

4. Toolbar

The **Toolbar** provides quick access to actions like running your app, debugging, creating new files, and managing virtual devices.

- **Run Button**: Launches your app on an emulator or physical device.
- **Build Button**: Compiles your code and builds the APK.
- **AVD Manager**: Opens the Android Virtual Device Manager to create and configure emulators.

5. Logcat

Logcat is the console output window where Android logs events, errors, and debug messages from your app. Logcat is essential for debugging, as it shows real-time information about what's happening while your app runs.

- **Filter by Tag**: Allows you to search for specific tags or keywords in the log.
- **Severity Levels**: You can filter messages by severity level, such as Debug (D), Error (E), and Info (I).
- **Logcat Commands**: You can use commands to clear or save logs, which is helpful when troubleshooting issues.

6. Gradle Panel

Gradle is Android's build automation tool, used to compile your code, manage dependencies, and create different build configurations. The **Gradle Panel** allows you to execute Gradle tasks and manage build settings.

- **Build Variants**: Allows you to switch between different build configurations, such as debug and release versions.
- **Dependencies**: Gradle handles dependencies, so you can easily add external libraries to your project by updating the build.gradle files.

Creating and Managing Projects

Android Studio simplifies the process of creating, opening, and managing projects. Let's go through the basics of each task.

Creating a New Project

1. From the Android Studio welcome screen, select **Start a new Android Studio project**.
2. Choose a project template. Templates provide different starting points, such as a blank activity, navigation drawer, or tabbed activity.
3. Configure your project:
    - **Name**: Enter a name for your project.

- **Package Name**: Unique identifier for your app, typically in reverse domain notation (e.g., com.example.myapp).
- **Save Location**: Choose where to store the project files.
- **Language**: Choose **Kotlin** or **Java**.
- **Minimum API Level**: Set the minimum Android version your app will support.

Click **Finish** to create your project, and Android Studio will open it in the editor.

Opening an Existing Project

1. From the welcome screen, select **Open an existing Android Studio project**.
2. Browse to the location of the project and select the root folder (the one containing app and build.gradle files).
3. Click **OK** to open the project in Android Studio.

Alternatively, if you already have a project open, you can go to **File > Open...** to select and open a new project.

Managing Project Settings

In Android Studio, you can manage your project settings through the **Project Structure** dialog and the build.gradle files.

- **Project Structure (File > Project Structure)**: Allows you to manage project-level and module-level settings, including dependencies, SDK versions, and build configurations.
- **build.gradle Files**: The project-level build.gradle file manages overall project settings, while the app-level build.gradle file manages settings specific to the app module, such as dependencies and build types.

Renaming a Project

To rename a project:

1. Close the project in Android Studio and navigate to the project directory on your computer.
2. Rename the folder containing the project files.
3. Open the project in Android Studio by selecting the renamed folder.

Tip: Be cautious when renaming packages or classes within the project, as they may have references in multiple files.

Debugging Basics: Using Debugging Tools and Logcat

Debugging is a critical skill in software development, and Android Studio provides powerful tools to help you find and fix issues in your code. In this section, we'll introduce some of the core debugging features in Android Studio, including breakpoints, the debugger, and Logcat.

1. Using Breakpoints

Breakpoints allow you to pause your app's execution at specific lines of code, so you can inspect variables and analyze the program's flow.

- **Setting a Breakpoint**: Click in the left margin next to a line of code in the Code Editor. A red dot will appear, indicating the breakpoint.
- **Running with the Debugger**: Click the **Debug** button (a bug icon) on the toolbar to start your app in debug mode. The app will pause at each breakpoint.
- **Inspecting Variables**: When the app is paused, hover over variables to see their current values. The **Variables** pane displays all variable states in the current context.
- **Step Over/Into**: Use the **Step Over** and **Step Into** buttons to control the flow of execution line-by-line, allowing you to carefully examine each part of the code.

2. Using Logcat

Logcat is an invaluable tool for viewing real-time logs and debugging messages. Log statements provide a record of events and errors while the app is running, helping you track down issues without stopping the app.

Adding Log Statements:

- In your Kotlin code, you can use the Log class to print messages to the Logcat. This class provides methods to log messages at different levels:

  ```kotlin
  kotlin
  import android.util.Log

  Log.d("MainActivity", "This is a debug message")
  Log.e("MainActivity", "This is an error message")
  ```

  Log Levels:

  - **Verbose (V)**: Shows all logs, including detailed information.
  - **Debug (D)**: Shows debugging information, useful for development.
  - **Info (I)**: Shows general-purpose information messages.
  - **Warning (W)**: Indicates potential problems that don't affect app functionality.
  - **Error (E)**: Logs errors that prevent certain functionality from working correctly.

Filtering Logs:

- In the Logcat panel, you can filter logs by tag, level, or keyword to focus on specific messages. Filtering helps narrow down the log output, making it easier to find relevant information.

Clearing Logs:

- Click the **Clear Logcat** button to clear old logs, which can be useful when focusing on specific sections of the app.

3. Analyzing Crashes and Exceptions

When your app crashes, Logcat will display an error message (typically with the tag E/AndroidRuntime) that includes details about the crash. The stack trace shows the lines of code that led to the error, allowing you to pinpoint the cause.

1. Look for the line labeled Caused by, which usually indicates the main reason for the crash.
2. Locate the line number and file in the stack trace to find the code responsible for the crash.
3. Use breakpoints and Logcat to reproduce and analyze the issue, so you can fix it effectively.

In this chapter, we explored the core features of Android Studio, including its panels, tools, and file structure. We covered how to create, open, and manage projects, and introduced essential debugging tools like breakpoints and Logcat.

By mastering the basics of Android Studio, you're now equipped to navigate, organize, and troubleshoot your projects with confidence. In the next chapter, we'll dive into Kotlin programming essentials, the language used for modern Android development, so you can start writing and understanding the code that powers Android apps.

CHAPTER 4: INTRODUCTION TO KOTLIN FOR ANDROID DEVELOPMENT

Kotlin has become the preferred language for Android development due to its modern syntax, safety features, and compatibility with Java. This chapter will introduce you to the basics of Kotlin, including syntax for variables, functions, conditionals, and loops. By the end of this chapter, you'll be comfortable with Kotlin's fundamentals and ready to start coding Android applications.

Why Kotlin?

Kotlin vs. Java

Kotlin was officially adopted as the preferred language for Android development by Google in 2017. Although Java is still widely supported, Kotlin offers several advantages that make it particularly suited for modern app development.

1. **Concise and Readable**: Kotlin's syntax is more concise than Java, reducing the amount of code needed to accomplish the same tasks. This improves code readability and reduces the likelihood of errors.
2. **Null Safety**: NullPointerExceptions are a common source of errors in Java. Kotlin addresses this with built-in null

safety features, helping developers avoid unexpected crashes.

3. **Interoperability with Java**: Kotlin is fully interoperable with Java, meaning you can use Kotlin and Java side by side in the same project. This allows you to gradually transition from Java to Kotlin or use Java libraries with Kotlin code.
4. **Enhanced Features**: Kotlin includes advanced features like extension functions, data classes, and lambda expressions that enable more expressive and flexible code.

Why Kotlin is Ideal for Android Development

Kotlin's features make it easier and faster to write code that is both powerful and reliable. With tools and resources provided by Google and JetBrains, Kotlin is highly integrated into Android Studio, offering excellent support for building Android apps.

Basic Kotlin Syntax

Let's explore the fundamentals of Kotlin, including how to declare variables, write functions, use conditionals, and create loops. This section will give you the foundation to write simple programs in Kotlin and use it effectively in Android development.

1. Variables

Kotlin variables are declared with either val or var:

- **val**: Immutable (read-only) variable. Once assigned, its value cannot be changed.
- **var**: Mutable variable. You can change its value.

Example:

```kotlin
val greeting: String = "Hello, Kotlin" // Immutable variable
var age: Int = 25 // Mutable variable

// Type inference allows omitting the type if it's obvious
val name = "John"
var score = 100
```

In Kotlin, you don't have to specify the type explicitly if it can be inferred. The compiler determines the type based on the assigned value.

2. Functions

Functions in Kotlin are defined using the fun keyword. Functions can return values, have parameters, and use default values.

Example:

```kotlin
// Function with no parameters and a return value
fun sayHello(): String {
    return "Hello, Kotlin"
}
```

```
// Function with parameters and a return value
fun addNumbers(a: Int, b: Int): Int {
   return a + b
}

// Function with a default parameter
fun greet(name: String = "Guest") {
   println("Hello, $name!")
}

// Calling functions
println(sayHello()) // Outputs: Hello, Kotlin
println(addNumbers(5, 10)) // Outputs: 15
greet("Alice") // Outputs: Hello, Alice!
greet() // Outputs: Hello, Guest!
```

Kotlin also supports **single-expression functions**. When a function only has a single expression, it can be written more concisely:

```kotlin
fun multiply(a: Int, b: Int) = a * b
```

3. Conditionals

Kotlin's if and when expressions allow you to handle conditional logic.

if Expression: The if statement in Kotlin can also be used as an expression, meaning it can return a value.

```kotlin
val number = 10
val isEven = if (number % 2 == 0) "Even" else "Odd"
println(isEven) // Outputs: Even
```

when Expression: The when expression is Kotlin's more powerful version of switch in other languages. It's useful for checking multiple conditions.

```kotlin
val score = 85
val grade = when (score) {
    in 90..100 -> "A"
    in 80..89 -> "B"
    in 70..79 -> "C"
    else -> "F"
}
println(grade) // Outputs: B
```

4. Loops

Kotlin provides several ways to loop through data, including for loops and while loops.

for Loop: You can loop through ranges, arrays, or collections with for.

```kotlin
// Looping through a range
for (i in 1..5) {
    println(i) // Outputs numbers from 1 to 5
}

// Looping through an array
val fruits = arrayOf("Apple", "Banana", "Cherry")
for (fruit in fruits) {
    println(fruit)
}
```

while and do-while Loops: while loops repeat a block of code as long as a condition is true, while do-while loops execute at least once before checking the condition.

```kotlin
var count = 5
while (count > 0) {
    println(count) // Outputs: 5 4 3 2 1
    count--
}
```

Working with Kotlin in Android

Now that we've covered basic Kotlin syntax, let's see how to use Kotlin in an Android project. In Android Studio, Kotlin is fully integrated, so you can use it to write activity classes, manipulate UI components, and handle user interactions.

Creating a Simple App with Kotlin

Let's create a basic app that displays a welcome message and responds to a button click using Kotlin.

Step 1: Set Up the Project

1. Start a new project in Android Studio, select **Empty Activity**, and choose **Kotlin** as the language.
2. Set the project name to "KotlinDemo" and configure the rest of the settings, then click **Finish**.

Step 2: Modify the Layout (activity_main.xml) In your project's res/layout/activity_main.xml, update the layout to include a TextView and a Button.

```
xml
<?xml version="1.0" encoding="utf-8"?>
<LinearLayout
xmlns:android="http://schemas.android.com/apk/res/android"
   android:layout_width="match_parent"
   android:layout_height="match_parent"
   android:orientation="vertical"
   android:gravity="center"
   android:padding="16dp">
```

```
    <TextView
        android:id="@+id/welcomeText"
        android:layout_width="wrap_content"
        android:layout_height="wrap_content"
        android:text="Welcome to Kotlin!"
        android:textSize="24sp"
        android:padding="16dp" />

    <Button
        android:id="@+id/changeTextButton"
        android:layout_width="wrap_content"
        android:layout_height="wrap_content"
        android:text="Change Text" />
</LinearLayout>
```

Step 3: Write the Kotlin Code in MainActivity.kt In MainActivity.kt, you'll write code to update the text in the TextView when the button is clicked.

```
kotlin
package com.example.kotlindemo

import android.os.Bundle
import androidx.appcompat.app.AppCompatActivity
import android.widget.Button
import android.widget.TextView
```

```
class MainActivity : AppCompatActivity() {

  override fun onCreate(savedInstanceState: Bundle?) {
    super.onCreate(savedInstanceState)
    setContentView(R.layout.activity_main)

    // Find the TextView and Button by their IDs
    val welcomeText: TextView = findViewById(R.id.welcomeText)
    val changeTextButton: Button = findViewById(R.id.changeTextButton)

    // Set an OnClickListener for the Button
    changeTextButton.setOnClickListener {
      welcomeText.text = "Text changed with Kotlin!"
    }
  }
}
```

Explanation:

- **findViewById**: This method links the TextView and Button in the XML layout to Kotlin variables in the activity. The findViewById function locates a view by its ID.

- **OnClickListener**: The setOnClickListener function is used to define an action when the button is clicked. In this case, it changes the TextView text to a new message.

Step 4: Run the App

1. Click the **Run** button in Android Studio.
2. Select an emulator or a physical device to install and run the app.
3. Once the app launches, tap the "Change Text" button to see the TextView text update.

You've just created a basic interactive app using Kotlin!

In this chapter, you learned why Kotlin is the preferred language for Android development and explored its basic syntax, including variables, functions, conditionals, and loops. You then applied your knowledge by creating a simple Android app in Kotlin that changes text on a button click.

Kotlin's concise and safe syntax makes it a powerful language for Android development. Now that you're familiar with Kotlin basics, you're ready to start working with core Android components. In the next chapter, we'll dive into Android app fundamentals, including activities, the activity lifecycle, and how to structure an Android application.

CHAPTER 5: ANDROID APP FUNDAMENTALS

To create functional and responsive Android applications, it's essential to understand the foundational components and architecture that make up an Android app. In this chapter, we'll explore the core components of an Android application, learn about the activity lifecycle, and discuss the architecture of Android apps. By the end, you'll have a solid understanding of how Android apps are structured and how each component plays a role in the app's functionality.

Understanding Android Components

Android applications are built using four primary components. Each component serves a unique purpose and works together to create an interactive and seamless experience for the user.

1. Activities

An **Activity** represents a single screen in an Android app. It's where the user interacts with the app's UI and performs tasks. Activities handle the display of layouts and respond to user interactions like button clicks or text input. Each app can have one or more activities, depending on the number of screens or tasks it needs.

- **Example**: In a messaging app, the main screen showing recent conversations might be one activity, while the chat screen displaying messages with a particular contact could be another activity.

2. Services

A **Service** is a component that runs in the background to perform long-running operations without interacting with the user. Services are useful for tasks that need to continue even if the user navigates away from the app's UI.

- **Types of Services**:
    - **Started Service**: Runs until it completes its task or is stopped manually.
    - **Bound Service**: Binds to other app components, allowing them to interact with the service. It runs as long as there is a bound component.

- **Example**: In a music app, a service can handle music playback in the background, allowing the user to continue listening while browsing other screens or using other apps.

3. Broadcast Receivers

A **Broadcast Receiver** allows your app to listen for system-wide broadcast announcements. These broadcasts can be triggered by the system (e.g., low battery, incoming call) or by other applications. When a specific event occurs, the broadcast receiver responds by taking an action, such as notifying the user or starting another component.

- **Example**: A weather app might use a broadcast receiver to check for changes in connectivity to update weather data when the device reconnects to the internet.

4. Content Providers

A **Content Provider** is used to manage shared data that can be accessed by multiple applications. It provides a way to access structured data and share it across different apps in a secure way. Content providers use a URI (Uniform Resource Identifier) to allow access to specific data.

- **Example**: Android's built-in Contacts app provides a content provider to share contact information. Other apps, like messaging or social media apps, can access contacts through this content provider.

Activity Lifecycle

Understanding the **Activity Lifecycle** is essential because it allows you to manage the activity's behavior as the user navigates through the app. The lifecycle is managed by a series of callback methods that the system invokes as the user's interaction with the activity changes.

1. Lifecycle Callbacks

Here's a breakdown of the main lifecycle methods and what each does:

- **onCreate()**: Called when the activity is first created. This is where you initialize resources, set up UI components, and prepare the activity for display.
- **onStart()**: Called when the activity becomes visible to the user but isn't yet ready for interaction.
- **onResume()**: Called when the activity is ready to interact with the user. It's the foreground activity, and this is where the app runs in full force.
- **onPause()**: Called when the system is about to resume another activity. Use this method to save unsaved data or pause animations and other CPU-heavy tasks.
- **onStop()**: Called when the activity is no longer visible to the user, either because another activity has taken over the screen or the activity is being closed. Release resources that don't need to remain active while the activity isn't visible.

- **onRestart()**: Called if the activity was stopped and is now restarting. Useful for preparing the activity to enter the foreground again.
- **onDestroy()**: Called when the activity is finishing or being destroyed by the system. Free up all resources and perform final cleanup here.

2. Lifecycle Example: A Simple Activity Lifecycle Flow

Consider a messaging app:

- When the user opens the app, onCreate() initializes resources, and onResume() displays the UI for reading messages.
- If the user receives a call, onPause() is called to pause any active processes, and onStop() saves the message draft as the app moves out of focus.
- Once the call ends, onRestart() and onResume() bring the app back into focus, resuming the UI.

Here's a simplified visual flow:

1. **Activity is created**: onCreate() → onStart() → onResume().
2. **User switches to another app**: onPause() → onStop().
3. **User returns to the app**: onRestart() → onStart() → onResume().
4. **User closes the app**: onPause() → onStop() → onDestroy().

This lifecycle flow allows developers to handle the user's navigation smoothly, ensuring that resources are managed properly and that the app responds to changes in visibility.

Application Architecture

Android apps are structured around multiple layers and components, making them modular and scalable. Let's look at the core elements of Android app architecture.

1. Manifest File

The **AndroidManifest.xml** file is the configuration file for your app. It defines essential information about your app, including its package name, the activities and services it contains, and the permissions it needs.

- **Components**: Declares each activity, service, broadcast receiver, and content provider in the app.
- **Permissions**: Specifies any permissions the app needs, such as internet access or location permissions.
- **Intent Filters**: Defines which activities can respond to specific types of intents, enabling deep linking or launching the app for specific actions.

Example:

xml

```
<manifest
xmlns:android="http://schemas.android.com/apk/res/android"
  package="com.example.myapp">

  <application
    android:allowBackup="true"
    android:label="MyApp"
    android:icon="@mipmap/ic_launcher">

    <!-- Main activity -->
    <activity android:name=".MainActivity">
      <intent-filter>
        <action android:name="android.intent.action.MAIN" />
        <category
android:name="android.intent.category.LAUNCHER" />
      </intent-filter>
    </activity>

  </application>
</manifest>
```

2. Application Class

The **Application class** serves as the entry point for the app and is instantiated when the app starts. It allows you to maintain global app state and perform initialization tasks that only need to happen once, like setting up analytics or configuring libraries.

To create an Application class, extend android.app.Application and register it in the manifest file:

```kotlin
class MyApp : Application() {
    override fun onCreate() {
        super.onCreate()
        // Initialize librariès or settings here
    }
}
```

In AndroidManifest.xml:

```xml
<application
    android:name=".MyApp"
    android:label="MyApp"
    android:icon="@mipmap/ic_launcher">
    ...
</application>
```

3. MVVM (Model-View-ViewModel) Architecture

Modern Android apps often use the **MVVM (Model-View-ViewModel)** pattern to organize code in a way that promotes separation of concerns and testability.

- **Model**: Represents the data layer. It's responsible for data handling, network operations, and database management.

- **View**: Represents the UI layer. Activities and fragments are part of the view layer and are responsible for displaying data to the user.
- **ViewModel**: Acts as a bridge between the Model and View. It manages UI-related data in a lifecycle-aware manner and provides data to the view via LiveData or other observable data structures.

MVVM makes it easier to write modular code that's easier to maintain and test. Here's a quick breakdown of each layer:

- **Model**: Handles data operations (e.g., fetching data from a network or database).
- **ViewModel**: Holds the data for the view, observes changes, and updates the view when data changes.
- **View**: Displays the data and interacts with the user, sending actions back to the ViewModel.

Example of MVVM Flow

1. The **View** (e.g., MainActivity) displays a list of items.
2. The **ViewModel** fetches the data through the **Model** and updates the view when the data is ready.
3. When the user interacts with the data (e.g., clicking an item), the action is handled by the ViewModel, which updates the Model.

In this chapter, you learned about the core components of an Android app—activities, services, broadcast receivers, and content providers. We explored the activity lifecycle, which dictates how an activity behaves as the user navigates through the app, and introduced Android app architecture, including the AndroidManifest.xml file, the Application class, and the MVVM pattern.

With these foundational concepts in place, you're ready to start building Android applications with a clear understanding of how each part works. In the next chapter, we'll dive into building user interfaces with XML, where you'll learn to create layouts and design the visual structure of your app.

CHAPTER 6: BUILDING USER INTERFACES WITH XML

In Android development, XML (Extensible Markup Language) is used to design and structure the user interface. XML allows you to define elements visually and arrange them in layouts that dictate how an app appears to users. In this chapter, we'll introduce XML layouts, go over common UI elements like TextView, Button, and ImageView, and walk through creating a simple layout using XML. By the end, you'll have the knowledge to create basic interfaces for your Android applications.

Introduction to XML Layouts

What is XML?

XML is a markup language that structures data in a hierarchical format, using tags to define elements. In Android, XML is used to define UI layouts, allowing developers to specify the position, appearance, and behavior of UI components. XML files in Android are stored in the res/layout directory and are separate from the Kotlin or Java code.

Why XML for UI Design?

Using XML for UI design has several benefits:

- **Separation of Concerns**: XML keeps the UI separate from application logic, making it easier to update the UI without changing the code.
- **Readability**: XML's tag-based structure makes it easy to understand the hierarchy and relationships between UI components.
- **Compatibility with Various Devices**: XML layouts can adapt to different screen sizes and resolutions, making it easier to create responsive UIs.

XML Layout Structure

In Android, each layout XML file starts with a root element that contains child elements (UI components). The root element often defines the structure of the layout, while each child element represents a UI component.

Example:

xml

```
<?xml version="1.0" encoding="utf-8"?>
<LinearLayout
xmlns:android="http://schemas.android.com/apk/res/android"
    android:layout_width="match_parent"
    android:layout_height="match_parent"
    android:orientation="vertical">

    <TextView
        android:layout_width="wrap_content"
        android:layout_height="wrap_content"
        android:text="Hello, World!" />

</LinearLayout>
```

In this example, LinearLayout is the root element, and TextView is a child element. Each UI component has attributes like layout_width, layout_height, and others to control its appearance and behavior.

Basic UI Elements

Android provides several common UI elements that form the building blocks of most apps. Let's explore some of the most frequently used elements.

1. TextView

TextView displays text on the screen. It's a basic element used to show static content, such as labels or messages.

Example:

```xml
<TextView
    android:layout_width="wrap_content"
    android:layout_height="wrap_content"
    android:text="Welcome to Android"
    android:textSize="18sp"
    android:textColor="#000000" />
```

Attributes:

- android:text: Sets the text content.
- android:textSize: Controls the text size (in sp, which scales with user font settings).
- android:textColor: Sets the text color (in hexadecimal format).

2. Button

Button is an interactive UI element that users can click to trigger an action, such as submitting a form or navigating to another screen.

Example:

```xml
<Button
    android:layout_width="wrap_content"
```

```
   android:layout_height="wrap_content"
   android:text="Click Me"
   android:onClick="onButtonClick" />
```

Attributes:

- android:text: Sets the button label.
- android:onClick: Defines a method to handle the button click in the code (e.g., onButtonClick in MainActivity).

3. EditText

EditText allows users to enter and edit text input, such as typing in a username or password. It's commonly used in forms and login screens.

Example:

xml

```
<EditText
   android:layout_width="match_parent"
   android:layout_height="wrap_content"
   android:hint="Enter your name"
   android:inputType="textPersonName" />
```

Attributes:

- android:hint: Provides a hint when the field is empty.
- android:inputType: Specifies the type of input (e.g., text, number, email, etc.).

4. ImageView

ImageView displays an image, which can be from local resources or an external URL (when loaded programmatically). It's used to display logos, icons, photos, and other visual content.

Example:

```xml
<ImageView
    android:layout_width="100dp"
    android:layout_height="100dp"
    android:src="@drawable/ic_launcher_foreground"
    android:contentDescription="App Logo" />
```

Attributes:

- android:src: Sets the image source (from the res/drawable directory).
- android:contentDescription: Provides a description for accessibility (e.g., screen readers).

5. CheckBox and RadioButton

- **CheckBox**: Allows users to select multiple options independently.
- **RadioButton**: Allows users to select a single option from a set.

Example:

```xml
<CheckBox
    android:layout_width="wrap_content"
    android:layout_height="wrap_content"
    android:text="Subscribe to newsletter" />

<RadioGroup
    android:layout_width="wrap_content"
    android:layout_height="wrap_content">

    <RadioButton
        android:layout_width="wrap_content"
        android:layout_height="wrap_content"
        android:text="Option 1" />

    <RadioButton
        android:layout_width="wrap_content"
        android:layout_height="wrap_content"
        android:text="Option 2" />
</RadioGroup>
```

Designing Simple Layouts

Now that we've covered some basic UI elements, let's create a simple layout with XML. In this layout, we'll include a welcome message, an input field, and a button.

Step 1: Open the Layout XML File

1. In Android Studio, navigate to res/layout and open activity_main.xml.
2. Set the root element to a LinearLayout with vertical orientation, so elements stack on top of each other.

Step 2: Add UI Components

Here's a sample XML code for a simple layout:

xml

Copy code

```
<?xml version="1.0" encoding="utf-8"?>
<LinearLayout
xmlns:android="http://schemas.android.com/apk/res/android"
    android:layout_width="match_parent"
    android:layout_height="match_parent"
    android:orientation="vertical"
    android:padding="16dp">

    <!-- TextView for welcome message -->
    <TextView
        android:layout_width="wrap_content"
        android:layout_height="wrap_content"
        android:text="Welcome to Android Development"
        android:textSize="24sp"
```

```
    android:textColor="#3F51B5"
    android:layout_gravity="center" />

  <!-- EditText for user input -->
  <EditText
    android:id="@+id/usernameEditText"
    android:layout_width="match_parent"
    android:layout_height="wrap_content"
    android:hint="Enter your name"
    android:inputType="textPersonName"
    android:marginTop="16dp" />

  <!-- Button to submit input -->
  <Button
    android:id="@+id/submitButton"
    android:layout_width="wrap_content"
    android:layout_height="wrap_content"
    android:text="Submit"
    android:layout_gravity="center"
    android:marginTop="16dp" />

</LinearLayout>
```

Explanation:

- TextView: Displays a welcome message with customized text size and color.

- EditText: Provides a field for the user to enter their name, with a hint.
- Button: A button labeled "Submit" that will eventually handle user input (we'll connect it to functionality in the next chapters).

Step 3: Adjust Layout Attributes

- layout_width and layout_height define the size of each element:
    - **match_parent**: Makes the element as large as its parent container.
    - **wrap_content**: Sizes the element to fit its content.
- orientation="vertical": In LinearLayout, this stacks elements vertically.
- padding and marginTop: Add space inside and around the elements for a more polished appearance.

Step 4: Run the Layout in the Emulator

1. Click the **Run** button in Android Studio.
2. Select your virtual device or a connected physical device.
3. You should see a simple screen with a welcome message, an input field, and a button.

This layout demonstrates how XML makes it easy to structure a UI visually and specify the appearance of each element.

In this chapter, you learned the basics of XML layout design in Android, including the structure of XML files, the role of XML in separating the UI from the code, and the purpose of common UI elements like TextView, Button, EditText, and ImageView. We also walked through the creation of a simple layout using XML, giving you a hands-on example of how to structure and customize a basic Android interface.

With these skills, you're ready to start designing more complex and interactive user interfaces. In the next chapter, we'll explore more advanced layout techniques, including view groups and organizing views in different layouts, so you can create responsive and flexible designs for various screen sizes.

CHAPTER 7: USING VIEWS AND LAYOUTS

Building an effective and user-friendly Android app requires a solid understanding of views, layouts, and responsive design. In this chapter, we'll explore view groups like LinearLayout, RelativeLayout, and ConstraintLayout, discuss best practices for structuring views, and introduce the concept of responsive design to create layouts that adapt to different screen sizes and orientations. By the end of this chapter, you'll be able to organize UI components effectively and build layouts that look great on any device.

Understanding View Groups

In Android, view groups are container elements that hold and organize UI components (or child views). Each view group has a unique way of arranging its children, allowing you to create a structured layout that meets the design needs of your app.

Here are the most commonly used view groups:

1. LinearLayout

LinearLayout arranges its child views in a single row or column, either horizontally or vertically. It's a simple and efficient layout for stacking elements.

- **Orientation**: You can set android:orientation to horizontal or vertical to control the layout direction.
- **Weight Attribute**: layout_weight allows you to distribute space proportionally between child views, giving you flexibility over the layout's appearance.

Example:

```xml
<LinearLayout
    android:layout_width="match_parent"
    android:layout_height="match_parent"
    android:orientation="vertical">

    <TextView
        android:layout_width="wrap_content"
        android:layout_height="wrap_content"
        android:text="Hello, World!" />

    <Button
        android:layout_width="wrap_content"
        android:layout_height="wrap_content"
```

```
    android:text="Click Me" />
</LinearLayout>
```

2. RelativeLayout

RelativeLayout allows you to position child views relative to each other or to the parent container. It offers more flexibility than LinearLayout for complex arrangements.

- **Relative Positioning**: Use attributes like layout_alignParentTop, layout_below, layout_toRightOf, and layout_centerInParent to place views relative to other views or the parent.

Example:

```xml
<RelativeLayout
  android:layout_width="match_parent"
  android:layout_height="match_parent">

  <TextView
    android:id="@+id/label"
    android:layout_width="wrap_content"
    android:layout_height="wrap_content"
    android:text="Username" />

  <EditText
```

```
    android:layout_width="match_parent"
    android:layout_height="wrap_content"
    android:layout_below="@id/label"
    android:layout_marginTop="8dp"
    android:hint="Enter your username" />
</RelativeLayout>
```

3. ConstraintLayout

ConstraintLayout is the most versatile layout in Android and is recommended for building complex, responsive UIs. It allows you to define constraints between views, creating flexible layouts that adapt well to different screen sizes.

- **Positioning with Constraints**: You can constrain views relative to the parent container, other views, or guidelines. This allows for more advanced alignment and positioning options.
- **Guidelines and Chains**: ConstraintLayout includes tools like horizontal/vertical guidelines and chains to organize elements consistently.

Example:

xml

```
<androidx.constraintlayout.widget.ConstraintLayout
  android:layout_width="match_parent"
  android:layout_height="match_parent">
```

```
    <TextView
        android:id="@+id/welcomeText"
        android:layout_width="wrap_content"
        android:layout_height="wrap_content"
        android:text="Welcome"
        app:layout_constraintTop_toTopOf="parent"
        app:layout_constraintStart_toStartOf="parent"
        app:layout_constraintEnd_toEndOf="parent" />

    <Button
        android:id="@+id/startButton"
        android:layout_width="wrap_content"
        android:layout_height="wrap_content"
        android:text="Get Started"
        app:layout_constraintTop_toBottomOf="@id/welcomeText"
        app:layout_constraintStart_toStartOf="parent"
        app:layout_constraintEnd_toEndOf="parent"
        app:layout_constraintBottom_toBottomOf="parent" />
</androidx.constraintlayout.widget.ConstraintLayout>
```

In this example, ConstraintLayout positions TextView at the top center of the screen and places the Button directly below it, also centered.

4. Other Layouts

- **FrameLayout**: A simple layout that stacks children on top of each other, where each view overlaps the previous one.
- **GridLayout**: Arranges child views in a grid with rows and columns. Useful for creating grid-based layouts.

Organizing Views: Best Practices for Structuring Views for Different Screen Sizes

When structuring views in your layout, it's essential to consider design principles that make your app adaptable and efficient. Here are some best practices:

1. Use Nested Layouts Sparingly

While nesting layouts (placing one view group inside another) can help achieve complex designs, too many nested layouts slow down rendering and impact performance. Use ConstraintLayout when possible, as it reduces the need for deeply nested views.

2. Leverage Layout Parameters and Attributes

Each view group and view has various attributes that can control their behavior and appearance. Understanding and effectively using these attributes will improve layout efficiency.

- **layout_width** and **layout_height**: match_parent fills the available space in the parent, while wrap_content sizes the view to its content.

- **layout_weight** (LinearLayout): Controls the distribution of space between elements in LinearLayout.
- **layout_margin** and **padding**: Use margin to control the space around views and padding to control space within views.

3. Design for Multiple Orientations

Consider how your layout will look in both portrait and landscape orientations. In landscape mode, the screen width is greater than the height, so rearrange views to fit the space better. You can define different layouts for portrait and landscape by creating separate layout folders (res/layout for portrait and res/layout-land for landscape).

4. Consider Accessibility

Designing accessible layouts ensures that all users, including those with disabilities, can use your app. Use descriptive contentDescription attributes for images, consider font sizes, and test your layout with screen readers to improve accessibility.

5. Test on Multiple Devices

Testing your app on various screen sizes and densities (e.g., small, medium, large, extra-large) helps ensure that your layout is adaptable and looks good on all Android devices. The Android emulator and Android Studio's Layout Editor offer previews for different screen sizes.

Creating Responsive Layouts

Responsive design is about creating layouts that adapt gracefully to different screen sizes, resolutions, and orientations. Android provides various tools and techniques for building responsive UIs.

1. Use Density-Independent Pixels (dp) and Scalable Pixels (sp)

- **dp** (density-independent pixels) is a unit that scales with screen density, ensuring that UI elements appear the same size on all devices.
- **sp** (scale-independent pixels) is used for text size and scales according to user preferences. Using sp ensures that text is readable for users with different display settings.

Example:

```xml
<TextView
    android:layout_width="wrap_content"
    android:layout_height="wrap_content"
    android:text="Hello, World!"
    android:textSize="18sp"
    android:padding="16dp" />
```

2. Create Alternative Layouts

Android allows you to create alternative layouts based on screen size and orientation. By creating specific layout folders with qualifiers, you can customize layouts for different screen configurations.

- **res/layout**: Default layout for regular screens.
- **res/layout-large**: Layout for large screens, such as tablets.
- **res/layout-sw600dp**: Layout for screens with a minimum width of 600dp.
- **res/layout-land**: Layout for landscape orientation.

Example: Creating a different layout for tablets

1. In the res folder, create a new folder named layout-large.
2. Copy the activity_main.xml file into layout-large.
3. Customize this layout file to optimize it for larger screens.

When your app runs on a large screen, Android will automatically load the layout from layout-large, ensuring an optimized user experience.

3. Use ConstraintLayout for Flexible Positioning

ConstraintLayout is ideal for creating responsive layouts because of its constraint-based positioning system. Constraints make it possible to define relationships between elements that adapt to screen size changes.

- **Percent Constraints**: Use percentage-based constraints to position elements in relation to the parent's size.

- **Chains**: Chains allow you to position views horizontally or vertically within a layout, distributing space evenly or weighted.

4. Utilize Android's Resource Qualifiers for Responsiveness

Resource qualifiers help Android choose the right resources (such as layouts, images, or dimensions) based on the device's characteristics. For example:

- **Screen Size**: layout-sw600dp for tablets, layout-small for smaller screens.
- **Orientation**: layout-land for landscape, layout-port for portrait.
- **Density**: Use drawable folders like drawable-mdpi, drawable-hdpi, drawable-xhdpi to provide different image resolutions for varying screen densities.

5. Flexible Images and Graphics

For images, provide multiple resolutions so they look crisp on all devices. Use vector graphics (.xml files in the drawable folder) for icons and scalable images, as they resize without losing quality. Vector graphics adjust automatically to screen sizes and densities, making them an excellent choice for a responsive UI.

Example: Creating a Responsive Layout with ConstraintLayout

Let’s create a responsive layout that includes a title, an image, and a button. We’ll use ConstraintLayout to position these elements flexibly.

xml

Copy code

```
<androidx.constraintlayout.widget.ConstraintLayout
xmlns:android="http://schemas.android.com/apk/res/android"
    android:layout_width="match_parent"
    android:layout_height="match_parent">

    <TextView
        android:id="@+id/titleText"
        android:layout_width="wrap_content"
        android:layout_height="wrap_content"
        android:text="Welcome to My App"
        android:textSize="24sp"
        app:layout_constraintTop_toTopOf="parent"
        app:layout_constraintStart_toStartOf="parent"
        app:layout_constraintEnd_toEndOf="parent"
        android:padding="16dp" />

    <ImageView
        android:id="@+id/sampleImage"
        android:layout_width="0dp"
        android:layout_height="0dp"
```

```
    android:src="@drawable/sample_image"
    app:layout_constraintTop_toBottomOf="@id/titleText"
    app:layout_constraintStart_toStartOf="parent"
    app:layout_constraintEnd_toEndOf="parent"
    app:layout_constraintDimensionRatio="H,1:1" />

  <Button
    android:id="@+id/getStartedButton"
    android:layout_width="wrap_content"
    android:layout_height="wrap_content"
    android:text="Get Started"
    app:layout_constraintTop_toBottomOf="@id/sampleImage"
    app:layout_constraintStart_toStartOf="parent"
    app:layout_constraintEnd_toEndOf="parent"
    android:marginTop="16dp" />

</androidx.constraintlayout.widget.ConstraintLayout>
```

In this layout:

- The TextView is positioned at the top center.
- The ImageView is centered below the title, with a 1:1 aspect ratio.
- The Button is centered below the image.

With ConstraintLayout, this layout will adapt well to different screen sizes and orientations.

In this chapter, you learned about view groups (LinearLayout, RelativeLayout, ConstraintLayout) and best practices for organizing views, such as minimizing nested layouts and testing for different screen sizes. We also covered responsive design techniques using dp, sp, alternative layouts, and ConstraintLayout to build adaptive UIs.

Now that you understand layouts and responsive design, you're ready to start handling user interactions in your app. In the next chapter, we'll explore user interaction and event handling to make your app more dynamic and interactive.

CHAPTER 8: USER INTERACTION AND EVENT HANDLING

In Android apps, capturing user input and responding to events is fundamental to creating interactive and engaging experiences. In this chapter, we'll cover how to handle user input, use event listeners like click and touch events, and walk through practical examples, such as button clicks and form submissions. By the end, you'll be able to make your Android apps more dynamic by responding to various user actions.

Handling User Input

Capturing user input involves gathering data from UI elements like buttons, text fields, checkboxes, and more. These inputs help make your app interactive and responsive to user actions.

1. Buttons

Buttons are among the most common UI elements for capturing user input. When a user taps a button, an event is triggered, allowing the app to perform specific actions, such as navigating to a new screen or displaying a message.

Example:

xml

Copy code

```
<Button
    android:id="@+id/submitButton"
    android:layout_width="wrap_content"
    android:layout_height="wrap_content"
    android:text="Submit" />
```

2. Text Fields (EditText)

EditText is a versatile input field that lets users enter text, numbers, passwords, and other types of input. Android provides input types (such as text, number, email, etc.) to tailor the input field for specific uses.

Example:

xml

```
<EditText
    android:id="@+id/nameEditText"
    android:layout_width="match_parent"
    android:layout_height="wrap_content"
```

```
   android:hint="Enter your name"
   android:inputType="textPersonName" />
```

In this example, the EditText field prompts the user to enter their name. Setting android:inputType="textPersonName" restricts the keyboard to show inputs suited for a person's name.

3. CheckBoxes and RadioButtons

- **CheckBox**: Allows users to select or deselect multiple options independently.
- **RadioButton**: Allows users to select one option from a set of choices (typically grouped in a RadioGroup).

Example:

```xml
<CheckBox
   android:id="@+id/newsletterCheckBox"
   android:layout_width="wrap_content"
   android:layout_height="wrap_content"
   android:text="Subscribe to newsletter" />

<RadioGroup
   android:layout_width="wrap_content"
   android:layout_height="wrap_content">

   <RadioButton
```

```
        android:id="@+id/radioOption1"
        android:layout_width="wrap_content"
        android:layout_height="wrap_content"
        android:text="Option 1" />

    <RadioButton
        android:id="@+id/radioOption2"
        android:layout_width="wrap_content"
        android:layout_height="wrap_content"
        android:text="Option 2" />
</RadioGroup>
```

Using these components, you can capture various forms of user input and use that data to drive the behavior of your app.

Event Listeners

Event listeners allow your app to respond to user actions, such as clicks, swipes, or typing. By attaching event listeners to UI elements, you can control what happens when a user interacts with them.

1. Click Listeners

A **click listener** responds to user taps or clicks. The most common use of a click listener is with buttons, but it can also be applied to other views.

Example: In your activity file (e.g., MainActivity.kt), you can set up a click listener for a button.

```kotlin
val submitButton: Button = findViewById(R.id.submitButton)
submitButton.setOnClickListener {
    // Perform an action when the button is clicked
    Toast.makeText(this, "Button clicked!", Toast.LENGTH_SHORT).show()
}
```

In this example, when the button is clicked, a short message ("Button clicked!") will be displayed on the screen using a Toast message.

2. Text Change Listener

For EditText fields, a **text change listener** captures changes to the text as the user types. This can be helpful for real-time validations, search suggestions, or updating the UI dynamically based on user input.

Example:

```kotlin
val nameEditText: EditText = findViewById(R.id.nameEditText)
nameEditText.addTextChangedListener(object : TextWatcher {
    override fun afterTextChanged(s: Editable?) {
        // Code to run after text has changed
```

```
    }

    override fun beforeTextChanged(s: CharSequence?, start: Int, count: Int, after: Int) {
        // Code to run before text is changed
    }

    override fun onTextChanged(s: CharSequence?, start: Int, before: Int, count: Int) {
        // Code to run as text is changing
    }
})
```

The TextWatcher interface provides methods to handle changes at different stages: before, during, and after the text is modified.

3. Touch Events

Touch events allow you to detect and respond to more complex interactions, such as taps, swipes, or drags. The onTouchListener interface handles touch events, providing access to data like coordinates and event type.

Example:

kotlin

```
val imageView: ImageView = findViewById(R.id.imageView)
imageView.setOnTouchListener { view, event ->
    when (event.action) {
```

```
        MotionEvent.ACTION_DOWN -> {
            // Handle touch down event
            view.alpha = 0.5f
        }
        MotionEvent.ACTION_UP -> {
            // Handle touch up event
            view.alpha = 1.0f
        }
    }
    true
}
```

In this example, when the user touches the ImageView, its transparency changes to give visual feedback.

Practical Examples

Let's go through a few examples that combine user input and event handling to create interactive experiences.

Example 1: Button Click Event to Display Input

Let's create a simple app where the user enters their name in an EditText field, taps a button, and sees a personalized message displayed.

Step 1: Define the Layout in XML

```xml
<LinearLayout
```

```
xmlns:android="http://schemas.android.com/apk/res/android"
android:layout_width="match_parent"
android:layout_height="match_parent"
android:orientation="vertical"
android:padding="16dp">

<EditText
   android:id="@+id/nameEditText"
   android:layout_width="match_parent"
   android:layout_height="wrap_content"
   android:hint="Enter your name"
   android:inputType="textPersonName" />

<Button
   android:id="@+id/showMessageButton"
   android:layout_width="wrap_content"
   android:layout_height="wrap_content"
   android:text="Show Message" />

<TextView
   android:id="@+id/messageTextView"
   android:layout_width="wrap_content"
   android:layout_height="wrap_content"
   android:text=""
   android:textSize="18sp"
```

```
    android:paddingTop="16dp" />

</LinearLayout>
```

Step 2: Implement the Event Handling in Kotlin

In MainActivity.kt, capture the user input, respond to the button click, and display the personalized message.

```kotlin
val nameEditText: EditText = findViewById(R.id.nameEditText)
val showMessageButton: Button = findViewById(R.id.showMessageButton)
val messageTextView: TextView = findViewById(R.id.messageTextView)

showMessageButton.setOnClickListener {
    val name = nameEditText.text.toString()
    if (name.isNotEmpty()) {
        messageTextView.text = "Hello, $name!"
    } else {
        messageTextView.text = "Please enter your name."
    }
}
```

Explanation:

- The user enters their name in EditText.

- When the button is clicked, the app checks if the name field is empty.
- If not empty, it displays a personalized message in TextView; otherwise, it prompts the user to enter their name.

Example 2: Form Submission with Validation

Let's create a basic form where the user enters their email and password. When they click the "Submit" button, the app will validate the inputs and display a message indicating if the inputs are valid or not.

Step 1: Define the Layout in XML

```
xml
<LinearLayout
  xmlns:android="http://schemas.android.com/apk/res/android"
  android:layout_width="match_parent"
  android:layout_height="match_parent"
  android:orientation="vertical"
  android:padding="16dp">

  <EditText
    android:id="@+id/emailEditText"
    android:layout_width="match_parent"
    android:layout_height="wrap_content"
    android:hint="Email"
```

```
    android:inputType="textEmailAddress" />

  <EditText
    android:id="@+id/passwordEditText"
    android:layout_width="match_parent"
    android:layout_height="wrap_content"
    android:hint="Password"
    android:inputType="textPassword" />

  <Button
    android:id="@+id/submitButton"
    android:layout_width="wrap_content"
    android:layout_height="wrap_content"
    android:text="Submit" />

  <TextView
    android:id="@+id/feedbackTextView"
    android:layout_width="wrap_content"
    android:layout_height="wrap_content"
    android:text=""
    android:textColor="#FF0000"
    android:paddingTop="16dp" />

</LinearLayout>
```

Step 2: Implement the Event Handling and Validation in Kotlin

kotlin

Copy code

```
val emailEditText: EditText = findViewById(R.id.emailEditText)
val passwordEditText: EditText = findViewById(R.id.passwordEditText)
val submitButton: Button = findViewById(R.id.submitButton)
val feedbackTextView: TextView = findViewById(R.id.feedbackTextView)

submitButton.setOnClickListener {
  val email = emailEditText.text.toString()
  val password = passwordEditText.text.toString()

  if (email.isEmpty() || !android.util.Patterns.EMAIL_ADDRESS.matcher(email).matches()) {
    feedbackTextView.text = "Please enter a valid email."
  } else if (password.isEmpty() || password.length < 6) {
    feedbackTextView.text = "Password must be at least 6 characters long."
  } else {
    feedbackTextView.text = "Form submitted successfully!"
  }
```

```
}
```

Explanation:

- This example validates the email format and checks that the password has at least six characters.
- If the inputs are valid, it displays a success message. Otherwise, it displays an error message based on the missing or invalid input.

In this chapter, you learned how to handle user input using buttons, text fields, checkboxes, and radio buttons. We explored event listeners like click and touch events, allowing your app to respond dynamically to user interactions. Through practical examples, you built an interactive form and implemented validation to ensure input accuracy.

With these skills, you're ready to create more interactive features in your app. In the next chapter, we'll dive deeper into navigation and learn how to work with activities and intents, enabling your app to have multiple screens and enhanced functionality.

CHAPTER 9: WORKING WITH ACTIVITIES AND INTENTS

In Android development, activities and intents are key to building multi-screen apps. Activities represent individual screens, and intents facilitate navigation and communication between them. This chapter will introduce intents, show you how to pass data between activities, and provide a practical example of building a simple multi-screen app. By the end, you'll understand how to create and manage multiple screens and use intents to pass information across them.

Understanding Intents

An **intent** is a messaging object that Android uses to communicate between components, such as starting a new activity, sending a broadcast, or interacting with a service. Intents are essential for navigation in Android apps, as they allow you to launch new activities, move back and forth between screens, and send or receive data.

Types of Intents

1. **Explicit Intents**: Used to start a specific component by name (e.g., moving from one activity to another within the same app). This type of intent is common for intra-app navigation.
2. **Implicit Intents**: Used to perform an action without specifying a particular component. Android determines which component can handle the intent (e.g., opening a URL in a browser or sharing content).

Creating an Explicit Intent

To create an explicit intent and navigate to another activity, use the Intent class, passing the current context and the target activity class.

Example:

```kotlin
val intent = Intent(this, TargetActivity::class.java)
startActivity(intent)
```

This example creates an intent to navigate from the current activity to TargetActivity. When startActivity(intent) is called, Android launches TargetActivity, displaying the new screen.

Passing Data Between Activities

Often, you'll need to send data from one activity to another. Intents make it easy to pass key-value pairs with data between activities.

Adding Data to an Intent

You can add data to an intent using methods like putExtra, which associates a key with a value.

Example:

```kotlin
kotlin
val intent = Intent(this, TargetActivity::class.java)
intent.putExtra("USER_NAME", "John Doe")
startActivity(intent)
```

In this example, we attach a string value "John Doe" to the intent with the key "USER_NAME". You can pass various data types, including String, Int, Boolean, Parcelable, and more.

Retrieving Data in the Target Activity

In the target activity, retrieve the data by calling getIntent() and then using get methods with the same key used to put the data.

Example:

kotlin

val userName = intent.getStringExtra("USER_NAME")

If the key matches, getStringExtra("USER_NAME") retrieves the value associated with "USER_NAME". It's a good idea to check for null to handle cases where the data may be missing.

Practical Example: Building a Multi-Screen Information App

Let's build a simple information app where users can view details across multiple screens. In this example, we'll have two screens:

1. **MainActivity**: Displays a list of items.
2. **DetailActivity**: Shows details for a selected item.

Step 1: Setting Up the Project and Layouts

1. Create a New Project

Start a new project in Android Studio and name it something like "InfoApp." Use an empty activity as the template.

2. Define the Layout for MainActivity

In res/layout/activity_main.xml, create a layout that includes a TextView to display a list item and a Button to navigate to the detail screen.

```
xml
<?xml version="1.0" encoding="utf-8"?>
<LinearLayout
xmlns:android="http://schemas.android.com/apk/res/android"
```

```
    android:layout_width="match_parent"
    android:layout_height="match_parent"
    android:orientation="vertical"
    android:padding="16dp">

    <TextView
        android:id="@+id/itemTextView"
        android:layout_width="wrap_content"
        android:layout_height="wrap_content"
        android:text="Item 1: Introduction to Android"
        android:textSize="18sp"
        android:padding="8dp" />

    <Button
        android:id="@+id/detailButton"
        android:layout_width="wrap_content"
        android:layout_height="wrap_content"
        android:text="View Details" />
</LinearLayout>
```

In this layout:

- itemTextView displays a sample item.
- detailButton will navigate to the detail screen.

3. Define the Layout for DetailActivity

Create a new layout file named activity_detail.xml for the second screen.

```xml
<?xml version="1.0" encoding="utf-8"?>
<LinearLayout
xmlns:android="http://schemas.android.com/apk/res/android"
    android:layout_width="match_parent"
    android:layout_height="match_parent"
    android:orientation="vertical"
    android:padding="16dp">

    <TextView
        android:id="@+id/detailTextView"
        android:layout_width="wrap_content"
        android:layout_height="wrap_content"
        android:text="Detail Information"
        android:textSize="20sp" />

</LinearLayout>
```

In this layout:

- detailTextView will display detailed information about the selected item.

Step 2: Creating the Activities

1. MainActivity

In MainActivity, we'll set up a click listener on detailButton to start DetailActivity and pass data using an intent.

```kotlin
package com.example.infoapp

import android.content.Intent
import android.os.Bundle
import android.widget.Button
import android.widget.TextView
import androidx.appcompat.app.AppCompatActivity

class MainActivity : AppCompatActivity() {

    override fun onCreate(savedInstanceState: Bundle?) {
        super.onCreate(savedInstanceState)
        setContentView(R.layout.activity_main)

        val itemTextView: TextView = findViewById(R.id.itemTextView)
        val detailButton: Button = findViewById(R.id.detailButton)

        // Set up click listener for the button
        detailButton.setOnClickListener {
```

```
            val detailText = itemTextView.text.toString()
            val intent = Intent(this, DetailActivity::class.java)
            intent.putExtra("ITEM_DETAIL", detailText)
            startActivity(intent)
        }
    }
}
```

Explanation:

- The click listener on detailButton creates an intent to start DetailActivity.
- We use putExtra("ITEM_DETAIL", detailText) to attach the text from itemTextView as data to the intent.

2. DetailActivity

Create a new activity called DetailActivity and modify it to receive and display the data.

kotlin

```
package com.example.infoapp

import android.os.Bundle
import android.widget.TextView
import androidx.appcompat.app.AppCompatActivity

class DetailActivity : AppCompatActivity() {
```

```
    override fun onCreate(savedInstanceState: Bundle?) {
        super.onCreate(savedInstanceState)
        setContentView(R.layout.activity_detail)

        val detailTextView: TextView = findViewById(R.id.detailTextView)

        // Retrieve data passed from MainActivity
        val detailText = intent.getStringExtra("ITEM_DETAIL")
        detailTextView.text = detailText ?: "No details available"
    }
}
```

Explanation:

- getStringExtra("ITEM_DETAIL") retrieves the data sent from MainActivity.
- The data is displayed in detailTextView, or a default message is shown if no data is available.

Step 3: Run and Test the App

1. Click the **Run** button in Android Studio to launch the app on an emulator or physical device.
2. In the app, you'll see "Item 1: Introduction to Android" displayed on the main screen.

3. Tap the **View Details** button.
4. You should navigate to the detail screen, where the text "Item 1: Introduction to Android" is displayed.

Understanding the Flow

1. **MainActivity** displays a list item with a button.
2. When the button is clicked, it creates an intent, attaches data (the item text), and starts DetailActivity.
3. **DetailActivity** receives the data via the intent, retrieves it with getStringExtra, and displays it in detailTextView.

This structure allows you to build multi-screen apps that communicate between activities, providing a cohesive user experience.

In this chapter, you learned about intents and their role in navigation and communication in Android apps. We covered how to pass data between activities using intents, and you built a multi-screen information app with MainActivity and DetailActivity. Using intents, you can create more complex, interactive applications where users can navigate between screens seamlessly.

With these skills, you're ready to expand your apps with additional screens and data flow. In the next chapter, we'll explore fragments, which provide modular UI components within activities, allowing you to build more flexible and reusable layouts.

CHAPTER 10: FRAGMENTS FOR MODULAR UI DESIGN

Fragments are powerful UI components that allow for flexible, modular design within activities. They're useful for creating dynamic, multi-pane layouts and reusable sections within an app. In this chapter, we'll introduce fragments, cover how to create and use them within activities, and build an example tabbed interface using fragments. By the end of this chapter, you'll understand how to use fragments to create modular and dynamic user interfaces.

Introduction to Fragments

A **fragment** is a self-contained, reusable section of an app's UI that can be embedded within an activity. Fragments represent parts of the user interface within an activity, and they have their own lifecycle, similar to activities.

Why Use Fragments?

1. **Modular Design**: Fragments enable modular UI design, allowing you to split complex screens into smaller, manageable parts.
2. **Reusable Components**: You can reuse fragments across multiple activities, which saves development time and promotes consistency.
3. **Adaptive Layouts**: Fragments make it easy to create adaptive layouts for different screen sizes, especially useful for tablets and landscape orientation.
4. **Simplified Navigation**: Fragments can be used to switch content within an activity without needing to start a new activity, making navigation smoother and faster.

Fragment Lifecycle

Like activities, fragments have their own lifecycle with specific methods that the Android system calls as they're created, displayed, and destroyed. Here are the primary lifecycle methods:

- **onAttach()**: Called when the fragment is attached to its parent activity.
- **onCreateView()**: Called to initialize the fragment's user interface. This method returns the fragment's root view.
- **onViewCreated()**: Called immediately after onCreateView() to finalize the view setup.
- **onStart()** and **onResume()**: Called as the fragment becomes visible and active.
- **onPause()** and **onStop()**: Called as the fragment becomes partially or fully hidden.
- **onDestroyView()**: Called when the view hierarchy associated with the fragment is removed.
- **onDetach()**: Called when the fragment is detached from its parent activity.

Creating and Using Fragments

To create a fragment, you define a new class that extends Fragment. Each fragment has its own XML layout file for its UI. You can add a fragment to an activity programmatically or by defining it in the activity's XML layout.

1. Creating a Fragment

Let's start by creating a simple fragment that displays some text.

Step 1: Create the Fragment Class

Create a new Kotlin file, for example, ExampleFragment.kt, and extend it from Fragment.

```kotlin
package com.example.app

import android.os.Bundle
import android.view.LayoutInflater
import android.view.View
import android.view.ViewGroup
import androidx.fragment.app.Fragment

class ExampleFragment : Fragment() {

    override fun onCreateView(
        inflater: LayoutInflater, container: ViewGroup?,
        savedInstanceState: Bundle?
    ): View? {
        // Inflate the layout for this fragment
        return inflater.inflate(R.layout.fragment_example, container,
false)
    }
}
```

In this example, the onCreateView method inflates the layout for the fragment. We'll create the XML layout file (fragment_example.xml) in the next step.

Step 2: Define the Fragment's Layout

In the res/layout directory, create a new layout file named fragment_example.xml:

```xml
<?xml version="1.0" encoding="utf-8"?>
<LinearLayout
xmlns:android="http://schemas.android.com/apk/res/android"
    android:layout_width="match_parent"
    android:layout_height="match_parent"
    android:orientation="vertical"
    android:padding="16dp">

    <TextView
        android:layout_width="wrap_content"
        android:layout_height="wrap_content"
        android:text="This is an Example Fragment"
        android:textSize="18sp" />

</LinearLayout>
```

In this layout, we simply add a TextView to display a message.

2. Adding the Fragment to an Activity

You can add a fragment to an activity's layout statically (in XML) or dynamically (in code).

Static Fragment Addition

To add a fragment statically, include the <fragment> tag in the activity's XML layout file (e.g., activity_main.xml).

```xml
<?xml version="1.0" encoding="utf-8"?>
<LinearLayout
xmlns:android="http://schemas.android.com/apk/res/android"
   android:layout_width="match_parent"
   android:layout_height="match_parent"
   android:orientation="vertical">

   <fragment
      android:id="@+id/exampleFragment"
      android:name="com.example.app.ExampleFragment"
      android:layout_width="match_parent"
      android:layout_height="wrap_content" />

</LinearLayout>
```

In this approach, Android automatically adds the ExampleFragment to the activity when it's created.

Dynamic Fragment Addition

To add a fragment dynamically, use the FragmentManager and FragmentTransaction classes in your activity. This approach is more flexible, allowing you to add, remove, and replace fragments programmatically.

Example:

```kotlin
val fragment = ExampleFragment()
supportFragmentManager.beginTransaction()
    .replace(R.id.fragmentContainer, fragment)
    .commit()
```

In this example, the fragment is added to a container in the activity's layout (e.g., a FrameLayout with the ID fragmentContainer).

Example Project: Building a Tabbed Interface with Fragments

Let's create a tabbed interface that uses fragments to display different content on each tab.

Step 1: Setting Up the Project with Tab Layout

1. Create a new project in Android Studio with an **Empty Activity** template.
2. Open activity_main.xml and define a TabLayout and a ViewPager2 for navigation between tabs.

```xml
<?xml version="1.0" encoding="utf-8"?>
```

```
<LinearLayout
xmlns:android="http://schemas.android.com/apk/res/android"
    android:layout_width="match_parent"
    android:layout_height="match_parent"
    android:orientation="vertical">

    <com.google.android.material.tabs.TabLayout
        android:id="@+id/tabLayout"
        android:layout_width="match_parent"
        android:layout_height="wrap_content" />

    <androidx.viewpager2.widget.ViewPager2
        android:id="@+id/viewPager"
        android:layout_width="match_parent"
        android:layout_height="match_parent" />
</LinearLayout>
```

In this layout:

- TabLayout displays the tab titles.
- ViewPager2 allows swiping between fragments for each tab.

Step 2: Creating Fragment Classes for Each Tab

Create two simple fragment classes, Tab1Fragment and Tab2Fragment.

Tab1Fragment:

```kotlin
class Tab1Fragment : Fragment() {
    override fun onCreateView(
        inflater: LayoutInflater, container: ViewGroup?,
        savedInstanceState: Bundle?
    ): View? {
        return inflater.inflate(R.layout.fragment_tab1, container, false)
    }
}
```

Tab2Fragment:

```kotlin
class Tab2Fragment : Fragment() {
    override fun onCreateView(
        inflater: LayoutInflater, container: ViewGroup?,
        savedInstanceState: Bundle?
    ): View? {
        return inflater.inflate(R.layout.fragment_tab2, container, false)
    }
}
```

Next, define layouts for each fragment in fragment_tab1.xml and fragment_tab2.xml.

fragment_tab1.xml:

```xml
<LinearLayout
xmlns:android="http://schemas.android.com/apk/res/android"
    android:layout_width="match_parent"
    android:layout_height="match_parent"
    android:orientation="vertical"
    android:padding="16dp">

    <TextView
        android:layout_width="wrap_content"
        android:layout_height="wrap_content"
        android:text="This is Tab 1"
        android:textSize="18sp" />
</LinearLayout>
```

fragment_tab2.xml:

```xml
<LinearLayout
xmlns:android="http://schemas.android.com/apk/res/android"
    android:layout_width="match_parent"
    android:layout_height="match_parent"
    android:orientation="vertical"
    android:padding="16dp">
```

```
    <TextView
        android:layout_width="wrap_content"
        android:layout_height="wrap_content"
        android:text="This is Tab 2"
        android:textSize="18sp" />
</LinearLayout>
```

Step 3: Setting Up the ViewPager Adapter

Create a FragmentPagerAdapter for ViewPager2 to manage fragments for each tab.

```kotlin
class ViewPagerAdapter(activity: FragmentActivity) : FragmentStateAdapter(activity) {
    override fun getItemCount(): Int = 2 // Number of tabs

    override fun createFragment(position: Int): Fragment {
        return when (position) {
            0 -> Tab1Fragment()
            1 -> Tab2Fragment()
            else -> throw IllegalStateException("Unexpected position $position")
        }
    }
}
```

Step 4: Configuring Tab Layout in MainActivity

In MainActivity, set up the TabLayout with the ViewPager2 and configure the tabs.

kotlin

```
class MainActivity : AppCompatActivity() {

    override fun onCreate(savedInstanceState: Bundle?) {
        super.onCreate(savedInstanceState)
        setContentView(R.layout.activity_main)

        val viewPager: ViewPager2 = findViewById(R.id.viewPager)
        val tabLayout: TabLayout = findViewById(R.id.tabLayout)

        // Set up the ViewPager adapter
        viewPager.adapter = ViewPagerAdapter(this)

        // Attach the ViewPager to the TabLayout
        TabLayoutMediator(tabLayout, viewPager) { tab, position ->
            tab.text = when (position) {
                0 -> "Tab 1"
                1 -> "Tab 2"
                else -> null
            }
        }.attach()
    }
}
```

Here's what happens:

- ViewPagerAdapter provides fragments for each tab position.
- TabLayoutMediator links TabLayout and ViewPager2, setting tab titles based on position.

Step 5: Run the App

Click **Run** in Android Studio, and you should see two tabs labeled "Tab 1" and "Tab 2." Swiping or tapping on each tab displays the corresponding fragment content.

In this chapter, you learned about fragments and their role in modular UI design. We explored how to create and use fragments, both statically and dynamically. Finally, we built a tabbed interface using TabLayout and ViewPager2, demonstrating how fragments can be used to create a smooth, multi-pane user experience.

With fragments, you can create more adaptable and modular interfaces, perfect for complex and multi-functional apps. In the next chapter, we'll explore data storage and persistence, covering techniques for storing user data, so your app retains information across sessions.

CHAPTER 11: DATA STORAGE AND PERSISTENCE

Data storage and persistence allow Android apps to retain information even after the app is closed or the device is restarted. In this chapter, we'll explore different ways to store data in Android, focusing on SharedPreferences for small data storage, SQLite for structured data, and a practical example of building a simple note-taking app. By the end, you'll know how to use these storage options to build apps that retain user information across sessions.

Using SharedPreferences: Storing Small Amounts of Data

SharedPreferences is a simple and lightweight way to store key-value pairs in Android. It's ideal for saving small amounts of data, like user settings, preferences, and simple configurations.

When to Use SharedPreferences

- Saving user preferences (e.g., theme selection).
- Storing boolean flags (e.g., whether a user has completed onboarding).
- Saving small data points (e.g., a high score or last login time).

Working with SharedPreferences

SharedPreferences provides methods to read and write data, allowing you to store values such as String, Int, Boolean, Float, and Long.

Step 1: Creating or Accessing SharedPreferences

You can access SharedPreferences by calling getSharedPreferences() with a name and a mode.

kotlin

```
val sharedPreferences = getSharedPreferences("MyPrefs",
MODE_PRIVATE)
```

Step 2: Storing Data

To save data, use SharedPreferences.Editor to apply or commit changes.

kotlin

```
val editor = sharedPreferences.edit()
editor.putString("user_name", "John Doe")
editor.putInt("user_age", 25)
editor.apply() // or editor.commit() to save synchronously
```

Step 3: Retrieving Data

Retrieve stored values by providing a key and a default value.

kotlin

```
val userName = sharedPreferences.getString("user_name",
"Default Name")
val userAge = sharedPreferences.getInt("user_age", 0)
```

SQLite Database Basics: Setting Up and Using a SQLite Database

For structured data storage, SQLite is a powerful option. It allows you to store large amounts of data in a structured, queryable format. SQLite is well-suited for apps that need to manage complex data, like contact lists, notes, or product catalogs.

When to Use SQLite

- When you need to store and manage structured data.
- For complex queries or data manipulation.
- When data relationships are needed (like between tables).

Setting Up SQLite Database

To work with SQLite, you'll create a SQLiteOpenHelper class, which helps manage database creation, version management, and upgrades.

Step 1: Creating a Database Helper Class

Create a new Kotlin class, e.g., DatabaseHelper.kt, that extends SQLiteOpenHelper.

```kotlin
import android.content.Context
import android.database.sqlite.SQLiteDatabase
import android.database.sqlite.SQLiteOpenHelper
```

```
class DatabaseHelper(context: Context) :
SQLiteOpenHelper(context, DATABASE_NAME, null,
DATABASE_VERSION) {

  companion object {
    private const val DATABASE_NAME = "notes.db"
    private const val DATABASE_VERSION = 1

    // Table and columns
    const val TABLE_NAME = "notes"
    const val COLUMN_ID = "id"
    const val COLUMN_TITLE = "title"
    const val COLUMN_CONTENT = "content"
  }

  override fun onCreate(db: SQLiteDatabase) {
    val createTable = "CREATE TABLE $TABLE_NAME (" +
        "$COLUMN_ID INTEGER PRIMARY KEY
AUTOINCREMENT, " +
        "$COLUMN_TITLE TEXT, " +
        "$COLUMN_CONTENT TEXT)"
    db.execSQL(createTable)
  }
```

```
  override fun onUpgrade(db: SQLiteDatabase, oldVersion: Int,
newVersion: Int) {
      db.execSQL("DROP TABLE IF EXISTS $TABLE_NAME")
      onCreate(db)
  }
}
```

Explanation:

- onCreate(): Creates the notes table when the database is first created.
- onUpgrade(): Handles database schema changes by dropping the existing table and recreating it.

Step 2: Adding Data to the Database

Use insert to add data into the database. Here's how you can add a note with a title and content.

```kotlin
fun addNote(title: String, content: String): Long {
  val db = this.writableDatabase
  val values = ContentValues().apply {
      put(DatabaseHelper.COLUMN_TITLE, title)
      put(DatabaseHelper.COLUMN_CONTENT, content)
  }
  return db.insert(DatabaseHelper.TABLE_NAME, null, values)
}
```

Step 3: Retrieving Data from the Database

Use a Cursor to query data from the database.

kotlin

```
fun getAllNotes(): List<Note> {
   val notes = mutableListOf<Note>()
   val db = this.readableDatabase
   val cursor = db.query(DatabaseHelper.TABLE_NAME, null,
null, null, null, null, null)

   with(cursor) {
      while (moveToNext()) {
         val id =
getInt(getColumnIndexOrThrow(DatabaseHelper.COLUMN_ID))
         val title =
getString(getColumnIndexOrThrow(DatabaseHelper.COLUMN_T
ITLE))
         val content =
getString(getColumnIndexOrThrow(DatabaseHelper.COLUMN_C
ONTENT))
         notes.add(Note(id, title, content))
      }
   }
   cursor.close()
   return notes
```

```
}
```

In this example, we create a list of Note objects, with each note containing an id, title, and content.

Practical Example: Building a Simple Note-Taking App with Data Persistence

Let's put everything into practice by building a basic note-taking app that saves notes persistently using SQLite.

Step 1: Define the Note Data Class

Create a Kotlin data class to represent a note.

```
kotlin
data class Note(
    val id: Int = 0,
    val title: String,
    val content: String
)
```

Step 2: Set Up the MainActivity Layout

In activity_main.xml, create a layout with an EditText for the note title, a EditText for note content, a Button to save the note, and a RecyclerView to display saved notes.

```
xml
Copy code
<?xml version="1.0" encoding="utf-8"?>
```

```
<LinearLayout
xmlns:android="http://schemas.android.com/apk/res/android"
  android:layout_width="match_parent"
  android:layout_height="match_parent"
  android:orientation="vertical"
  android:padding="16dp">

  <EditText
    android:id="@+id/titleEditText"
    android:layout_width="match_parent"
    android:layout_height="wrap_content"
    android:hint="Note Title" />

  <EditText
    android:id="@+id/contentEditText"
    android:layout_width="match_parent"
    android:layout_height="wrap_content"
    android:hint="Note Content"
    android:layout_marginTop="8dp" />

  <Button
    android:id="@+id/saveButton"
    android:layout_width="wrap_content"
    android:layout_height="wrap_content"
    android:text="Save Note"
```

```
        android:layout_marginTop="8dp" />

    <androidx.recyclerview.widget.RecyclerView
        android:id="@+id/notesRecyclerView"
        android:layout_width="match_parent"
        android:layout_height="match_parent"
        android:layout_marginTop="16dp" />
</LinearLayout>
```

Step 3: Implementing the Note-Saving Functionality

In MainActivity, set up a click listener for the save button to save the note to the database.

kotlin

```
class MainActivity : AppCompatActivity() {
    private lateinit var databaseHelper: DatabaseHelper
    private lateinit var notesAdapter: NotesAdapter

    override fun onCreate(savedInstanceState: Bundle?) {
        super.onCreate(savedInstanceState)
        setContentView(R.layout.activity_main)

        databaseHelper = DatabaseHelper(this)

        val titleEditText: EditText =
findViewById(R.id.titleEditText)
```

```
    val contentEditText: EditText = findViewById(R.id.contentEditText)
    val saveButton: Button = findViewById(R.id.saveButton)
    val notesRecyclerView: RecyclerView = findViewById(R.id.notesRecyclerView)

    // Set up RecyclerView
    notesAdapter = NotesAdapter()
    notesRecyclerView.layoutManager = LinearLayoutManager(this)
    notesRecyclerView.adapter = notesAdapter

    loadNotes() // Load saved notes when the app starts

    // Save button click listener
    saveButton.setOnClickListener {
      val title = titleEditText.text.toString()
      val content = contentEditText.text.toString()
      if (title.isNotEmpty() && content.isNotEmpty()) {
        databaseHelper.addNote(title, content)
        titleEditText.text.clear()
        contentEditText.text.clear()
        loadNotes()
      } else {
```

```
            Toast.makeText(this, "Please enter a title and content", Toast.LENGTH_SHORT).show()
        }
    }
}

private fun loadNotes() {
    val notes = databaseHelper.getAllNotes()
    notesAdapter.setNotes(notes)
}
}
```

In this code:

- loadNotes() fetches all notes from the database and updates the RecyclerView.
- The save button's click listener saves a new note and refreshes the list.

Step 4: Creating a RecyclerView Adapter to Display Notes

Create a NotesAdapter class to display the list of notes.

```kotlin
class NotesAdapter : RecyclerView.Adapter<NotesAdapter.NoteViewHolder>() {

    private var notesList = mutableListOf<Note>()
```

```
  fun setNotes(notes: List<Note>) {
    this.notesList = notes.toMutableList()
    notifyDataSetChanged()
  }

  override fun onCreateViewHolder(parent: ViewGroup, viewType: Int): NoteViewHolder {
    val view = LayoutInflater.from(parent.context).inflate(R.layout.item_note, parent, false)
    return NoteViewHolder(view)
  }

  override fun onBindViewHolder(holder: NoteViewHolder, position: Int) {
    holder.bind(notesList[position])
  }

  override fun getItemCount(): Int = notesList.size

  class NoteViewHolder(itemView: View) : RecyclerView.ViewHolder(itemView) {
    private val titleTextView: TextView = itemView.findViewById(R.id.noteTitle)
```

```
    private val contentTextView: TextView = itemView.findViewById(R.id.noteContent)

    fun bind(note: Note) {
      titleTextView.text = note.title
      contentTextView.text = note.content
    }
  }
}
```

Create item_note.xml as the layout for each note item in the RecyclerView.

In this chapter, we covered two key data storage methods: SharedPreferences for small key-value data and SQLite for structured, relational data. We also built a practical note-taking app to demonstrate how to use SQLite for data persistence.

With these skills, you can now add data storage and persistence to your Android apps, ensuring they retain user information across sessions. In the next chapter, we'll dive into displaying lists with RecyclerView to manage and display larger collections of data effectively.

CHAPTER 12: RECYCLERVIEW AND LISTS

RecyclerView is one of the most powerful tools for displaying lists or grids of data in Android. It's designed to efficiently display large data sets by recycling views as they scroll off-screen. In this chapter, we'll introduce RecyclerView, explain how to set up adapters and view holders, and build an example project—a contact list that showcases how to use RecyclerView effectively.

Introduction to RecyclerView: Displaying Lists of Data Efficiently

RecyclerView is a flexible, efficient tool for displaying large lists or grids of items. Unlike ListView, which was commonly used in earlier versions of Android, RecyclerView offers improved performance, flexibility, and customization options.

Key Features of RecyclerView

1. **Efficient Memory Usage**: RecyclerView reuses view holders as they scroll off-screen, which reduces memory usage.
2. **Customizable Layouts**: You can arrange items in a list, grid, or custom layout using different layout managers.
3. **Flexible Animations**: RecyclerView allows you to add animations for items as they are added, removed, or updated.

Basic Structure of RecyclerView

A RecyclerView requires three main components:

- **Adapter**: Connects the data to the RecyclerView and manages the creation and binding of view holders.
- **ViewHolder**: Holds references to the item views and binds data to the views.
- **LayoutManager**: Manages the positioning and arrangement of items in the RecyclerView.

Creating Adapters and ViewHolders: Setting Up a RecyclerView

To display data in RecyclerView, you'll need to create an adapter and view holder to manage item views and data binding.

1. Setting Up the RecyclerView in Layout

Start by adding a RecyclerView in your activity's XML layout file (e.g., activity_main.xml).

```xml
<?xml version="1.0" encoding="utf-8"?>
<LinearLayout
xmlns:android="http://schemas.android.com/apk/res/android"
    android:layout_width="match_parent"
    android:layout_height="match_parent"
    android:orientation="vertical"
    android:padding="16dp">

    <androidx.recyclerview.widget.RecyclerView
```

```
        android:id="@+id/recyclerView"
        android:layout_width="match_parent"
        android:layout_height="match_parent" />
</LinearLayout>
```

2. Creating the Data Model

Define a data class that represents the data for each item in the list. For example, in a contact list, each contact might have a name and phone number.

```kotlin
data class Contact(
    val name: String,
    val phoneNumber: String
)
```

3. Creating the Layout for Each Item

Define the layout for each item in the list by creating a new XML layout file (e.g., item_contact.xml).

```xml
<?xml version="1.0" encoding="utf-8"?>
<LinearLayout
xmlns:android="http://schemas.android.com/apk/res/android"
    android:layout_width="match_parent"
    android:layout_height="wrap_content"
    android:orientation="vertical"
```

```
  android:padding="8dp">

  <TextView
    android:id="@+id/nameTextView"
    android:layout_width="wrap_content"
    android:layout_height="wrap_content"
    android:text="Name"
    android:textSize="18sp" />

  <TextView
    android:id="@+id/phoneTextView"
    android:layout_width="wrap_content"
    android:layout_height="wrap_content"
    android:text="Phone Number"
    android:textSize="16sp" />
</LinearLayout>
```

4. Creating the Adapter and ViewHolder

The adapter binds data to each item in the RecyclerView. It also creates view holders, which hold references to item views and are responsible for binding data to these views.

Step 1: Create a ViewHolder

A view holder represents a single item view in RecyclerView. It holds references to the views that display the data.

```kotlin
import android.view.View
import android.widget.TextView
import androidx.recyclerview.widget.RecyclerView

class ContactViewHolder(itemView: View) : RecyclerView.ViewHolder(itemView) {
    val nameTextView: TextView = itemView.findViewById(R.id.nameTextView)
    val phoneTextView: TextView = itemView.findViewById(R.id.phoneTextView)
}
```

Step 2: Create an Adapter

The adapter creates view holders and binds data to each item. Here's how to set up a basic adapter for the contact list:

```kotlin
import android.view.LayoutInflater
import android.view.View
import android.view.ViewGroup
import androidx.recyclerview.widget.RecyclerView

class ContactAdapter(private val contactList: List<Contact>) : RecyclerView.Adapter<ContactViewHolder>() {
```

```
  override fun onCreateViewHolder(parent: ViewGroup, viewType: Int): ContactViewHolder {
    val view = LayoutInflater.from(parent.context).inflate(R.layout.item_contact, parent, false)
    return ContactViewHolder(view)
  }

  override fun onBindViewHolder(holder: ContactViewHolder, position: Int) {
    val contact = contactList[position]
    holder.nameTextView.text = contact.name
    holder.phoneTextView.text = contact.phoneNumber
  }

  override fun getItemCount(): Int {
    return contactList.size
  }
}
```

Explanation:

- onCreateViewHolder: Inflates the item layout and creates a new ContactViewHolder.
- onBindViewHolder: Binds data to the views in ContactViewHolder for the specified position.
- getItemCount: Returns the number of items in the list.

Example Project: Building a Contact List App

Let's build a simple contact list app using RecyclerView. This app will display a list of contacts with their names and phone numbers.

Step 1: Define the MainActivity Layout

In activity_main.xml, add a RecyclerView to hold the list of contacts, as we did earlier.

```xml
<?xml version="1.0" encoding="utf-8"?>
<LinearLayout
xmlns:android="http://schemas.android.com/apk/res/android"
    android:layout_width="match_parent"
    android:layout_height="match_parent"
    android:orientation="vertical"
    android:padding="16dp">

    <androidx.recyclerview.widget.RecyclerView
        android:id="@+id/recyclerView"
        android:layout_width="match_parent"
        android:layout_height="match_parent" />
</LinearLayout>
```

Step 2: Implement MainActivity

In MainActivity, set up the RecyclerView, create sample data, and initialize the adapter.

```kotlin
import android.os.Bundle
import androidx.appcompat.app.AppCompatActivity
import androidx.recyclerview.widget.LinearLayoutManager
import androidx.recyclerview.widget.RecyclerView

class MainActivity : AppCompatActivity() {

    override fun onCreate(savedInstanceState: Bundle?) {
        super.onCreate(savedInstanceState)
        setContentView(R.layout.activity_main)

        // Sample contact data
        val contacts = listOf(
            Contact("Alice Johnson", "123-456-7890"),
            Contact("Bob Smith", "987-654-3210"),
            Contact("Carol White", "456-789-1234"),
            Contact("David Green", "321-654-9870"),
            Contact("Eva Brown", "789-123-4560")
        )

        // Set up RecyclerView
```

```
        val recyclerView: RecyclerView = findViewById(R.id.recyclerView)
        recyclerView.layoutManager = LinearLayoutManager(this)
        recyclerView.adapter = ContactAdapter(contacts)
    }
}
```

In this code:

- We create a list of Contact objects to use as sample data.
- We initialize the RecyclerView with a LinearLayoutManager to display items in a vertical list.
- We set the adapter of the RecyclerView to a new instance of ContactAdapter, passing in the list of contacts.

Step 3: Run the App

Run the app on an emulator or physical device. You should see a list of contacts, each displaying a name and a phone number. As you scroll, RecyclerView will recycle item views to save memory and improve performance.

Adding Click Events to RecyclerView Items

To make the contact list interactive, you can add a click listener to each item in the RecyclerView. Update the adapter to accept a click listener.

Step 1: Modify the Adapter to Accept a Click Listener

Add a clickListener parameter to the adapter constructor.

kotlin

```
class ContactAdapter(
  private val contactList: List<Contact>,
  private val clickListener: (Contact) -> Unit
) : RecyclerView.Adapter<ContactViewHolder>() {

  override fun onCreateViewHolder(parent: ViewGroup, viewType: Int): ContactViewHolder {
    val view = LayoutInflater.from(parent.context).inflate(R.layout.item_contact, parent, false)
    return ContactViewHolder(view)
  }

  override fun onBindViewHolder(holder: ContactViewHolder, position: Int) {
    val contact = contactList[position]
    holder.nameTextView.text = contact.name
    holder.phoneTextView.text = contact.phoneNumber
    holder.itemView.setOnClickListener { clickListener(contact)
}
  }

  override fun getItemCount(): Int = contactList.size
```

```
}
```

Step 2: Pass the Click Listener in MainActivity

In MainActivity, modify the adapter initialization to pass a click listener. For example, display a toast with the contact's name and phone number when clicked.

```
kotlin
import android.widget.Toast

// Inside onCreate()
recyclerView.adapter = ContactAdapter(contacts) { contact ->
  Toast.makeText(this, "Clicked: ${contact.name} - ${contact.phoneNumber}", Toast.LENGTH_SHORT).show()
}
```

Now, when you tap a contact in the list, a toast message appears showing the contact's details.

In this chapter, you learned how to use RecyclerView to display lists of data in Android. We covered setting up a RecyclerView, creating an adapter and view holder, and building a sample contact list app. Additionally, we explored adding click listeners to make items in the list interactive.

With RecyclerView, you can efficiently display and manage large collections of data, providing users with smooth, responsive list and grid experiences. In the next chapter, we'll explore networking basics, so you can connect your app to the internet and retrieve data from APIs, enhancing your app's functionality.

Chapter 13: Networking in Android

Networking allows Android apps to retrieve data from external sources, like web servers and APIs, making apps more dynamic and useful. In this chapter, we'll introduce HTTP and APIs, explain how to use Retrofit (a popular networking library) to make HTTP requests, and build a simple app that fetches data from a public API. By the end, you'll understand how to connect your Android app to the internet and retrieve data using Retrofit.

Introduction to HTTP and APIs

What is HTTP?

HTTP (Hypertext Transfer Protocol) is a protocol that defines how data is transmitted over the internet. In Android apps, HTTP is commonly used to retrieve or send data to web servers, typically through APIs (Application Programming Interfaces).

- **HTTP Request**: The app makes an HTTP request to a server (GET, POST, PUT, DELETE).
- **HTTP Response**: The server responds with data (e.g., JSON format), status code (e.g., 200 for success), and headers.

What is an API?

An **API** is a set of rules that allows an app to interact with an external service. APIs provide access to data and functionality on a server, enabling your app to retrieve information (like weather data) or perform actions (like sending messages).

- **RESTful API**: A popular type of API that uses standard HTTP methods (GET, POST, etc.) to retrieve or manipulate data.
- **JSON (JavaScript Object Notation)**: A lightweight data format often used for exchanging data between the server and the app.

Using Retrofit for Networking

Retrofit is a popular library in Android that simplifies the process of making HTTP requests and handling responses. It allows you to easily retrieve and parse JSON data into Kotlin or Java objects. Retrofit handles many networking complexities, making it a great choice for connecting Android apps to APIs.

Setting Up Retrofit in Android Studio

1. **Add Retrofit Dependency**: In build.gradle (app-level), add Retrofit and Gson dependencies to parse JSON.

   ```
   gradle
   dependencies {
       implementation 'com.squareup.retrofit2:retrofit:2.9.0'
   ```

```
implementation 'com.squareup.retrofit2:converter-gson:2.9.0'
}
```

2. **Sync the Project**: Click "Sync Now" to download and add the libraries to your project.

Basic Structure of a Retrofit Setup

To use Retrofit, you'll define:

1. **API Interface**: Defines the endpoints and request methods.
2. **Data Model**: Maps the JSON response to Kotlin data classes.
3. **Retrofit Instance**: Configures Retrofit with the base URL and converter.

1. Creating the API Interface

The API interface defines the endpoints your app can interact with. For example, let's define an API to fetch weather data using a GET request.

```kotlin
import retrofit2.Call
import retrofit2.http.GET
import retrofit2.http.Query

interface WeatherApiService {
```

```
    @GET("weather")
    fun getWeather(
        @Query("q") city: String,
        @Query("appid") apiKey: String
    ): Call<WeatherResponse>
}
```

In this example:

- @GET("weather"): Specifies a GET request to the /weather endpoint.
- @Query: Adds query parameters, such as q (city name) and appid (API key), to the request URL.
- WeatherResponse: Represents the JSON response, mapped to a Kotlin data class.

2. Creating the Data Model

Define data classes that represent the structure of the JSON response. Suppose the response contains the temperature and weather description:

```
json
{
    "main": {
        "temp": 280.32
    },
```

```
  "weather": [
    {
      "description": "clear sky"
    }
  ]
}
```

The corresponding data classes in Kotlin would be:

kotlin

```kotlin
data class WeatherResponse(
  val main: Main,
  val weather: List<WeatherDescription>
)

data class Main(
  val temp: Double
)

data class WeatherDescription(
  val description: String
)
```

3. Creating the Retrofit Instance

The Retrofit instance configures the base URL and specifies a converter (e.g., Gson) to parse JSON.

kotlin

```
import retrofit2.Retrofit
import retrofit2.converter.gson.GsonConverterFactory

object RetrofitInstance {
  private const val BASE_URL =
"https://api.openweathermap.org/data/2.5/"

  val api: WeatherApiService by lazy {
    Retrofit.Builder()
      .baseUrl(BASE_URL)
      .addConverterFactory(GsonConverterFactory.create())
      .build()
      .create(WeatherApiService::class.java)
  }
}
```

Practical Example: Building a Simple Weather App

Let's create a basic weather app that fetches weather data for a specific city using Retrofit. We'll use the OpenWeatherMap API (https://openweathermap.org/) as our data source.

Note: To use the OpenWeatherMap API, sign up for an API key (a unique identifier for making API requests).

Step 1: Set Up the Layout

In activity_main.xml, create a layout with an EditText to enter the city name, a Button to trigger the API request, and TextViews to display the temperature and description.

```xml
<?xml version="1.0" encoding="utf-8"?>
<LinearLayout
xmlns:android="http://schemas.android.com/apk/res/android"
    android:layout_width="match_parent"
    android:layout_height="match_parent"
    android:orientation="vertical"
    android:padding="16dp">

    <EditText
        android:id="@+id/cityEditText"
        android:layout_width="match_parent"
        android:layout_height="wrap_content"
        android:hint="Enter city name" />

    <Button
        android:id="@+id/fetchButton"
        android:layout_width="wrap_content"
        android:layout_height="wrap_content"
        android:text="Get Weather" />

    <TextView
```

```
        android:id="@+id/temperatureTextView"
        android:layout_width="wrap_content"
        android:layout_height="wrap_content"
        android:textSize="20sp"
        android:paddingTop="16dp" />

    <TextView
        android:id="@+id/descriptionTextView"
        android:layout_width="wrap_content"
        android:layout_height="wrap_content"
        android:textSize="20sp" />
</LinearLayout>
```

Step 2: Implement the MainActivity

In MainActivity, set up the button click listener to make the API call. Use RetrofitInstance to get the API interface and request weather data.

```kotlin
import android.os.Bundle
import android.widget.Button
import android.widget.EditText
import android.widget.TextView
import android.widget.Toast
import androidx.appcompat.app.AppCompatActivity
import retrofit2.Call
```

```
import retrofit2.Callback
import retrofit2.Response

class MainActivity : AppCompatActivity() {

  private val apiKey = "YOUR_API_KEY" // Replace with your
OpenWeatherMap API key

  override fun onCreate(savedInstanceState: Bundle?) {
    super.onCreate(savedInstanceState)
    setContentView(R.layout.activity_main)

    val cityEditText: EditText = findViewById(R.id.cityEditText)
    val fetchButton: Button = findViewById(R.id.fetchButton)
    val temperatureTextView: TextView =
findViewById(R.id.temperatureTextView)
    val descriptionTextView: TextView =
findViewById(R.id.descriptionTextView)

    fetchButton.setOnClickListener {
      val city = cityEditText.text.toString()
      if (city.isNotEmpty()) {
        fetchWeatherData(city, temperatureTextView,
descriptionTextView)
      } else {
```

```
            Toast.makeText(this, "Please enter a city name", Toast.LENGTH_SHORT).show()
        }
      }
    }

  private fun fetchWeatherData(city: String, temperatureTextView: TextView, descriptionTextView: TextView) {
      val call = RetrofitInstance.api.getWeather(city, apiKey)

      call.enqueue(object : Callback<WeatherResponse> {
        override fun onResponse(call: Call<WeatherResponse>, response: Response<WeatherResponse>) {
          if (response.isSuccessful) {
            val weatherResponse = response.body()
            val temperature = weatherResponse?.main?.temp?.minus(273.15)?.toInt() // Convert Kelvin to Celsius
            val description = weatherResponse?.weather?.get(0)?.description

            temperatureTextView.text = "Temperature: $temperature°C"
```

```
            descriptionTextView.text = "Description: $description"
        } else {
            Toast.makeText(this@MainActivity, "Failed to retrieve data", Toast.LENGTH_SHORT).show()
        }
    }

    override fun onFailure(call: Call<WeatherResponse>, t: Throwable) {
        Toast.makeText(this@MainActivity, "Error: ${t.message}", Toast.LENGTH_SHORT).show()
    }
  })
 }
}
```

Explanation:

- **fetchWeatherData()**: Makes the API request using Retrofit's enqueue method to handle the request asynchronously.
- **onResponse**: Checks if the response is successful, then retrieves and displays the temperature and description.
- **onFailure**: Handles errors by showing a toast message.

Testing the App

1. Run the app on an emulator or physical device.
2. Enter a city name (e.g., "London") in the EditText and tap **Get Weather**.
3. The app should display the current temperature and weather description for the specified city.

n this chapter, you learned about HTTP, APIs, and how to fetch data from a web server using Retrofit in Android. We covered the basics of Retrofit, including setting up an API interface, defining data models, and creating a Retrofit instance. Finally, we built a practical weather app that retrieves and displays data from a public API.

With these networking skills, you can now create Android apps that retrieve dynamic content from the internet, opening up a world of possibilities for interactive and up-to-date experiences. In the next chapter, we'll explore background tasks and services, which allow your app to perform tasks outside the main UI thread, such as background data fetching and notifications.

CHAPTER 14: WORKING WITH IMAGES AND MULTIMEDIA

Multimedia is a key aspect of many Android applications, as it enables apps to present visual and auditory information to users. In this chapter, we'll explore how to work with images, audio, and video in Android. We'll learn how to load images from the internet using libraries like Glide or Picasso, handle media files for playing audio and video, and build a simple example project that showcases these skills.

Loading Images with Glide or Picasso

Displaying images from the internet can be challenging due to factors like image size, caching, and performance. Glide and Picasso are popular image-loading libraries that handle these complexities, allowing you to load and display images efficiently.

Setting Up Glide or Picasso

1. **Add Glide Dependency** (recommended for its advanced features and high performance):

```
gradle
dependencies {
    implementation 'com.github.bumptech.glide:glide:4.12.0'
    annotationProcessor
'com.github.bumptech.glide:compiler:4.12.0'
}
```

Or Add Picasso Dependency:

```
gradle
dependencies {
    implementation 'com.squareup.picasso:picasso:2.71828'
}
```

2. **Sync the Project**: Click "Sync Now" in Android Studio to add the libraries.

Loading an Image with Glide

Glide is efficient for loading, caching, and displaying images from URLs, resources, and files.

```
kotlin
import com.bumptech.glide.Glide

val imageView: ImageView = findViewById(R.id.imageView)
Glide.with(this)
    .load("https://example.com/image.jpg")
```

```
    .placeholder(R.drawable.placeholder) // optional placeholder while loading
    .error(R.drawable.error_image)        // optional error image if loading fails
    .into(imageView)
```

Loading an Image with Picasso

Picasso is simple and efficient for basic image-loading tasks.

kotlin

```
import com.squareup.picasso.Picasso

val imageView: ImageView = findViewById(R.id.imageView)
Picasso.get()
    .load("https://example.com/image.jpg")
    .placeholder(R.drawable.placeholder) // optional placeholder
    .error(R.drawable.error_image)       // optional error image
    .into(imageView)
```

Both Glide and Picasso handle image caching, reducing load time and saving data.

Playing Audio and Video

Android provides APIs for playing audio and video, allowing you to create multimedia experiences. We'll use MediaPlayer for audio playback and VideoView for video playback in this section.

Playing Audio with MediaPlayer

The MediaPlayer class allows you to play audio files from resources, URLs, or local files.

1. **Load and Prepare Audio**: To play audio, create a MediaPlayer instance and specify the audio source.

   kotlin

   Copy code

   ```
   val mediaPlayer = MediaPlayer.create(this, R.raw.sample_audio)
   ```

   Or Load from URL:

   kotlin

   ```
   val mediaPlayer = MediaPlayer()
   mediaPlayer.setDataSource("https://example.com/sample_audio.mp3")
   mediaPlayer.prepare() // Prepares the player asynchronously
   ```

2. **Control Playback**: You can use methods to control playback: start() to play, pause() to pause, and stop() to stop the audio.

   kotlin

   ```
   mediaPlayer.start() // Play
   mediaPlayer.pause() // Pause
   mediaPlayer.stop()  // Stop
   ```

3. **Release Resources**: Always release MediaPlayer resources when done to avoid memory leaks.

```kotlin
mediaPlayer.release()
```

Playing Video with VideoView

VideoView is a simple and convenient way to play video files. It supports playing video from resources, local files, or URLs.

1. **Add a VideoView in Layout**:

```xml
<VideoView
    android:id="@+id/videoView"
    android:layout_width="match_parent"
    android:layout_height="match_parent" />
```

2. **Play Video in Code**:

```kotlin
val videoView: VideoView = findViewById(R.id.videoView)
videoView.setVideoPath("https://example.com/sample_video.mp4")
videoView.start()
```

3. **Using Media Controls**: Add media controls to VideoView for play, pause, and seek functionality.

```kotlin
val mediaController = MediaController(this)
videoView.setMediaController(mediaController)
mediaController.setAnchorView(videoView)
```

Note: Video streaming requires network permissions in AndroidManifest.xml:

```xml
<uses-permission
android:name="android.permission.INTERNET"/>
```

Example Project: Creating a Simple Image Gallery

Let's build an example project where we use Glide to load and display a series of images in a RecyclerView, simulating a basic image gallery.

Step 1: Define the Layout for MainActivity

In activity_main.xml, add a RecyclerView to display the images.

```xml
<?xml version="1.0" encoding="utf-8"?>
<LinearLayout
xmlns:android="http://schemas.android.com/apk/res/android"
   android:layout_width="match_parent"
   android:layout_height="match_parent"
```

```
    android:orientation="vertical">

    <androidx.recyclerview.widget.RecyclerView
        android:id="@+id/recyclerView"
        android:layout_width="match_parent"
        android:layout_height="match_parent" />
</LinearLayout>
```

Step 2: Create the Image Item Layout

Create a layout file item_image.xml for each image in the gallery.

xml

```
<?xml version="1.0" encoding="utf-8"?>
<FrameLayout
xmlns:android="http://schemas.android.com/apk/res/android"
    android:layout_width="match_parent"
    android:layout_height="wrap_content"
    android:padding="8dp">

    <ImageView
        android:id="@+id/imageView"
        android:layout_width="match_parent"
        android:layout_height="200dp"
        android:scaleType="centerCrop" />
</FrameLayout>
```

Step 3: Create the RecyclerView Adapter

Create an adapter to manage and display the images using Glide.

kotlin

```
import android.view.LayoutInflater
import android.view.View
import android.view.ViewGroup
import android.widget.ImageView
import androidx.recyclerview.widget.RecyclerView
import com.bumptech.glide.Glide

class ImageAdapter(private val imageUrls: List<String>) :
RecyclerView.Adapter<ImageAdapter.ImageViewHolder>() {

  class ImageViewHolder(view: View) :
RecyclerView.ViewHolder(view) {
    val imageView: ImageView =
view.findViewById(R.id.imageView)
  }

  override fun onCreateViewHolder(parent: ViewGroup,
viewType: Int): ImageViewHolder {
    val view =
LayoutInflater.from(parent.context).inflate(R.layout.item_image,
parent, false)
    return ImageViewHolder(view)
  }
```

```
  override fun onBindViewHolder(holder: ImageViewHolder, position: Int) {
      val imageUrl = imageUrls[position]
      Glide.with(holder.itemView.context)
        .load(imageUrl)
        .placeholder(R.drawable.placeholder) // Optional placeholder
        .into(holder.imageView)
  }

  override fun getItemCount(): Int = imageUrls.size
}
```

Step 4: Implement MainActivity

In MainActivity, set up the RecyclerView with sample image URLs and the ImageAdapter.

```kotlin
import android.os.Bundle
import androidx.appcompat.app.AppCompatActivity
import androidx.recyclerview.widget.LinearLayoutManager
import androidx.recyclerview.widget.RecyclerView

class MainActivity : AppCompatActivity() {
```

```
    override fun onCreate(savedInstanceState: Bundle?) {
        super.onCreate(savedInstanceState)
        setContentView(R.layout.activity_main)

        val recyclerView: RecyclerView =
findViewById(R.id.recyclerView)
        recyclerView.layoutManager = LinearLayoutManager(this)

        // Sample image URLs
        val imageUrls = listOf(
            "https://example.com/image1.jpg",
            "https://example.com/image2.jpg",
            "https://example.com/image3.jpg",
            "https://example.com/image4.jpg"
        )

        recyclerView.adapter = ImageAdapter(imageUrls)
    }
}
```

In this example:

- imageUrls holds URLs to be displayed.
- ImageAdapter uses Glide to load each image in RecyclerView.

Step 5: Run the App

Run the app on an emulator or physical device. You should see an image gallery where each image loads from an online URL using Glide, and as you scroll, images are recycled efficiently.

In this chapter, you learned how to handle images and multimedia in Android apps. We explored how to use Glide or Picasso to load images from URLs, use MediaPlayer to play audio, and use VideoView for video playback. Finally, we created a basic image gallery app to showcase how to load images dynamically into a RecyclerView.

With these multimedia skills, you can enhance your Android apps by adding engaging visual and auditory experiences. In the next chapter, we'll explore notifications and how to keep users informed with alerts and updates, even when they're not actively using the app.

CHAPTER 15: LOCATION AND MAPS

Location-based features are essential for many Android apps, providing users with relevant information based on their location. This chapter will cover how to access location services to retrieve GPS data, integrate Google Maps into your app, and build a simple location-based project, such as a nearby restaurant finder. By the end, you'll be able to incorporate location and mapping features into your apps to create engaging, location-aware experiences.

Accessing Location Services: Basics of Retrieving GPS Data

Android provides location services that allow apps to obtain the user's current location using GPS, Wi-Fi, and cellular networks. To access location services, we'll use the **FusedLocationProviderClient** from the Google Play Services Location API.

Setting Up Location Permissions

To access the user's location, you need to request permissions in AndroidManifest.xml.

xml

```
<uses-permission
android:name="android.permission.ACCESS_FINE_LOCATION"
/>
<uses-permission
android:name="android.permission.ACCESS_COARSE_LOCATION" />
```

Note: Starting from Android 6.0 (API level 23), location permissions need to be requested at runtime.

Setting Up the FusedLocationProviderClient

1. **Initialize FusedLocationProviderClient**: This client provides simple APIs to access the device's last known location and to request location updates.

   ```kotlin
   import com.google.android.gms.location.FusedLocationProviderClient
   import com.google.android.gms.location.LocationServices

   lateinit var fusedLocationClient: FusedLocationProviderClient

   override fun onCreate(savedInstanceState: Bundle?) {
       super.onCreate(savedInstanceState)
   ```

```
    setContentView(R.layout.activity_main)

    fusedLocationClient =
LocationServices.getFusedLocationProviderClient(this)
}
```

2. **Request the Last Known Location**: Use getLastLocation() to get the most recent location. Ensure permissions are granted before calling this method.

```
kotlin
Copy code
if (ContextCompat.checkSelfPermission(this,
Manifest.permission.ACCESS_FINE_LOCATION) ==
PackageManager.PERMISSION_GRANTED) {
    fusedLocationClient.lastLocation.addOnSuccessListener
{ location: Location? ->
        location?.let {
            val latitude = it.latitude
            val longitude = it.longitude
            // Use the location data (latitude, longitude) here
        }
    }
} else {
```

```
    ActivityCompat.requestPermissions(this,
  arrayOf(Manifest.permission.ACCESS_FINE_LOCATION
  ), LOCATION_PERMISSION_REQUEST_CODE)
  }
```

Handling Runtime Permissions

Request location permissions at runtime and handle the user's response.

kotlin

```
override fun onRequestPermissionsResult(requestCode: Int,
permissions: Array<String>, grantResults: IntArray) {
  if (requestCode ==
LOCATION_PERMISSION_REQUEST_CODE &&
grantResults.isNotEmpty() && grantResults[0] ==
PackageManager.PERMISSION_GRANTED) {
    // Permission granted, retrieve location
  } else {
    // Permission denied, handle accordingly
  }
}
```

Using Google Maps in Your App

Google Maps is widely used in Android apps for displaying maps and markers, getting directions, and other location-based services. To integrate Google Maps, you'll need to add the **Google Maps SDK for Android** and obtain an API key.

Setting Up Google Maps

1. **Enable Google Maps SDK and Obtain an API Key**:
   - Go to the Google Cloud Console.
   - Create or select a project, then enable the "Maps SDK for Android."
   - Generate an API key and restrict it to "Maps SDK for Android."
2. **Add the API Key to AndroidManifest.xml**:

```
xml
<meta-data
    android:name="com.google.android.geo.API_KEY"
    android:value="YOUR_API_KEY_HERE" />
```

3. **Add Google Maps Dependency** in build.gradle (app-level):

```
gradle
dependencies {
    implementation 'com.google.android.gms:play-services-maps:17.0.0'
}
```

4. **Create a Map Layout**: In activity_main.xml, add a SupportMapFragment to display the map.

```
xml
```

Copy code

```
<fragment
   android:id="@+id/map"

android:name="com.google.android.gms.maps.SupportMap
Fragment"
   android:layout_width="match_parent"
   android:layout_height="match_parent" />
```

5. **Initialize Google Maps in MainActivity**:

   Implement OnMapReadyCallback in your activity to initialize the map when it's ready.

   kotlin

```
import
com.google.android.gms.maps.CameraUpdateFactory
import com.google.android.gms.maps.GoogleMap
import
com.google.android.gms.maps.OnMapReadyCallback
import
com.google.android.gms.maps.SupportMapFragment
import com.google.android.gms.maps.model.LatLng
import
com.google.android.gms.maps.model.MarkerOptions
```

```
class MainActivity : AppCompatActivity(),
OnMapReadyCallback {

  private lateinit var map: GoogleMap

  override fun onCreate(savedInstanceState: Bundle?) {
    super.onCreate(savedInstanceState)
    setContentView(R.layout.activity_main)

    val mapFragment =
supportFragmentManager.findFragmentById(R.id.map) as
SupportMapFragment
    mapFragment.getMapAsync(this)
  }

  override fun onMapReady(googleMap: GoogleMap) {
    map = googleMap

    // Move the camera to a default location (e.g., New
York City)
    val defaultLocation = LatLng(40.7128, -74.0060)

map.addMarker(MarkerOptions().position(defaultLocation)
.title("New York City"))
```

```
map.moveCamera(CameraUpdateFactory.newLatLngZoom
(defaultLocation, 10f))
    }
}
```

Example Project: Nearby Restaurant Finder

Now that you understand how to access location data and use Google Maps, let's build a basic app that finds nearby restaurants.

Note: To retrieve nearby places, use the Google Places API, which requires a billing-enabled Google Cloud account. Here, we'll focus on adding a marker to represent a nearby location.

Step 1: Define the Layout

Create activity_main.xml with a SupportMapFragment to display the map and a FloatingActionButton to trigger location requests.

```xml
<RelativeLayout
xmlns:android="http://schemas.android.com/apk/res/android"
  android:layout_width="match_parent"
  android:layout_height="match_parent">

  <fragment
    android:id="@+id/map"
```

```
android:name="com.google.android.gms.maps.SupportMapFragm
ent"
        android:layout_width="match_parent"
        android:layout_height="match_parent" />


<com.google.android.material.floatingactionbutton.FloatingAction
Button
        android:id="@+id/locationButton"
        android:layout_width="wrap_content"
        android:layout_height="wrap_content"
        android:layout_alignParentBottom="true"
        android:layout_alignParentEnd="true"
        android:layout_margin="16dp"
        android:src="@drawable/ic_location" />
</RelativeLayout>
```

Step 2: Implement MainActivity to Fetch Location and Update Map

1. **Initialize Google Maps and FusedLocationProviderClient.**
2. **Fetch the User's Location** on button click and update the map with a marker for a nearby restaurant.

```
kotlin
import android.Manifest
import android.content.pm.PackageManager
import android.os.Bundle
import android.widget.Toast
import androidx.appcompat.app.AppCompatActivity
import androidx.core.app.ActivityCompat
import
com.google.android.gms.location.FusedLocationProviderClient
import com.google.android.gms.location.LocationServices
import com.google.android.gms.maps.CameraUpdateFactory
import com.google.android.gms.maps.GoogleMap
import com.google.android.gms.maps.OnMapReadyCallback
import com.google.android.gms.maps.SupportMapFragment
import com.google.android.gms.maps.model.LatLng
import com.google.android.gms.maps.model.MarkerOptions
import
com.google.android.material.floatingactionbutton.FloatingActionB
utton

class MainActivity : AppCompatActivity(), OnMapReadyCallback
{

    private lateinit var map: GoogleMap
```

```
  private lateinit var fusedLocationClient: FusedLocationProviderClient
  private val LOCATION_PERMISSION_REQUEST_CODE = 1

  override fun onCreate(savedInstanceState: Bundle?) {
    super.onCreate(savedInstanceState)
    setContentView(R.layout.activity_main)

    fusedLocationClient = LocationServices.getFusedLocationProviderClient(this)

    val mapFragment = supportFragmentManager.findFragmentById(R.id.map) as SupportMapFragment
    mapFragment.getMapAsync(this)

    val locationButton: FloatingActionButton = findViewById(R.id.locationButton)
    locationButton.setOnClickListener {
      fetchLocationAndShowNearby()
    }
  }

  override fun onMapReady(googleMap: GoogleMap) {
    map = googleMap
```

```
  }

  private fun fetchLocationAndShowNearby() {
    if (ActivityCompat.checkSelfPermission(this,
Manifest.permission.ACCESS_FINE_LOCATION) !=
PackageManager.PERMISSION_GRANTED) {
      ActivityCompat.requestPermissions(this,
arrayOf(Manifest.permission.ACCESS_FINE_LOCATION),
LOCATION_PERMISSION_REQUEST_CODE)
      return
    }

    fusedLocationClient.lastLocation.addOnSuccessListener {
location ->
      if (location != null) {
        val userLatLng = LatLng(location.latitude,
location.longitude)

map.addMarker(MarkerOptions().position(userLatLng).title("Your
Location"))

map.moveCamera(CameraUpdateFactory.newLatLngZoom(userLa
tLng, 15f))

        // Example: Add a marker for a nearby restaurant
```

```
            val nearbyRestaurant = LatLng(location.latitude + 0.01, location.longitude + 0.01) // Mock nearby location

map.addMarker(MarkerOptions().position(nearbyRestaurant).title("Nearby Restaurant"))
        } else {
            Toast.makeText(this, "Unable to fetch location", Toast.LENGTH_SHORT).show()
        }
    }
  }

  override fun onRequestPermissionsResult(requestCode: Int, permissions: Array<String>, grantResults: IntArray) {
      if (requestCode == LOCATION_PERMISSION_REQUEST_CODE && grantResults.isNotEmpty() && grantResults[0] == PackageManager.PERMISSION_GRANTED) {
          fetchLocationAndShowNearby()
      } else {
          Toast.makeText(this, "Permission denied", Toast.LENGTH_SHORT).show()
      }
  }
}
```

Explanation:

- **fetchLocationAndShowNearby()**: Retrieves the user's location and adds a marker on the map. It also adds a mock marker for a nearby restaurant.
- **onMapReady()**: Initializes the map once it's ready to use.

In this chapter, you learned how to access location services and integrate Google Maps into an Android app. We covered setting up Google Maps, requesting the user's location, and adding markers on the map. Finally, we built a simple location-based app that shows the user's current location and a nearby restaurant marker.

With location and mapping skills, you can create apps that provide location-based information and experiences, from navigation to local recommendations. In the next chapter, we'll cover push notifications, which keep users engaged and informed, even when they're not actively using your app.

CHAPTER 16: NOTIFICATIONS AND BACKGROUND SERVICES

Notifications and background services are essential features for creating responsive and user-engaging Android apps. Notifications alert users to important updates, even when they're not actively using the app, while background services allow apps to perform tasks continuously or periodically without user interaction. In this chapter, we'll learn how to set up notifications, work with background services, and build an example project where the app sends reminders or news updates to users.

Setting Up Notifications: How to Create and Manage Notifications

Android notifications provide a way to display brief messages outside of an app's UI, allowing you to inform users of time-sensitive events, reminders, or updates.

Creating a Basic Notification

1. **Add Notification Permissions**: Since Android 13 (API 33), notifications require user permission.

```xml
<uses-permission
android:name="android.permission.POST_NOTIFICATIO
NS" />
```

2. **Request Notification Permission (API 33 and above)**: Use the following code in your activity's onCreate method for API 33+.

```kotlin
if (Build.VERSION.SDK_INT >=
Build.VERSION_CODES.TIRAMISU) {
    ActivityCompat.requestPermissions(this,
arrayOf(Manifest.permission.POST_NOTIFICATIONS),
NOTIFICATION_PERMISSION_REQUEST_CODE)
}
```

3. **Set Up Notification Channel**: Notification channels are required on Android 8.0 (API 26) and above to organize notifications into categories.

```kotlin
import android.app.NotificationChannel
import android.app.NotificationManager
```

```
import android.os.Build

private fun createNotificationChannel() {
  if (Build.VERSION.SDK_INT >= Build.VERSION_CODES.O) {
    val channelId = "reminder_channel"
    val channelName = "Reminders"
    val channelDescription = "Channel for reminders and updates"
    val importance = NotificationManager.IMPORTANCE_DEFAULT
    val channel = NotificationChannel(channelId, channelName, importance).apply {
      description = channelDescription
    }
    val notificationManager: NotificationManager = getSystemService(NotificationManager::class.java)

notificationManager.createNotificationChannel(channel)
  }
}
```

4. **Create and Display the Notification**: Use NotificationCompat.Builder to create a notification and NotificationManager to display it.

```kotlin
kotlin
import androidx.core.app.NotificationCompat
import androidx.core.app.NotificationManagerCompat

private fun showNotification(title: String, message: String)
{
    val channelId = "reminder_channel"
    val notificationId = 1
    val builder = NotificationCompat.Builder(this,
channelId)
        .setSmallIcon(R.drawable.ic_notification)
        .setContentTitle(title)
        .setContentText(message)

.setPriority(NotificationCompat.PRIORITY_DEFAULT)
        .setAutoCancel(true)

    with(NotificationManagerCompat.from(this)) {
        notify(notificationId, builder.build())
    }
}
```

5. **Call createNotificationChannel and showNotification**: Call createNotificationChannel in onCreate to set up the channel, and use showNotification when you want to display a notification.

Working with Services: Basics of Services for Background Tasks

Services allow Android apps to perform background tasks that continue running even when the user is not interacting with the app. Services are commonly used for tasks like fetching data, playing music, or sending notifications on a schedule.

Types of Services

1. **Foreground Service**: Runs a visible task with a notification, such as playing music.
2. **Background Service**: Runs in the background but has limitations in recent Android versions due to battery optimization.
3. **JobIntentService or WorkManager**: Recommended for background tasks that need to run periodically or under specific conditions (like network availability).

Creating a Simple Service

A service can be started using startService() and can keep running until it is stopped manually with stopSelf() or stopService().

Step 1: Create a Service Class

Extend the Service class and override onStartCommand to define the task.

kotlin

```
import android.app.Service
```

```
import android.content.Intent
import android.os.IBinder
import android.util.Log

class ReminderService : Service() {

    override fun onStartCommand(intent: Intent?, flags: Int, startId: Int): Int {
        // Start task: could be a timer, data fetch, etc.
        Log.d("ReminderService", "Service is running...")
        // Stop service after task completion
        stopSelf()
        return START_NOT_STICKY
    }

    override fun onBind(intent: Intent?): IBinder? = null
}
```

Step 2: Register the Service in AndroidManifest.xml

xml

Copy code

```
<service android:name=".ReminderService" />
```

Step 3: Start the Service

You can start the service by calling startService().

kotlin

```
val serviceIntent = Intent(this, ReminderService::class.java)
startService(serviceIntent)
```

Using WorkManager for Periodic Tasks

For tasks that need to run periodically or under specific conditions, WorkManager is a better choice. It's compatible with the system's battery and memory optimizations, making it ideal for recurring background tasks.

Example: Set up a WorkManager task to run periodically.

```kotlin
import androidx.work.PeriodicWorkRequestBuilder
import androidx.work.WorkManager
import androidx.work.Worker
import androidx.work.WorkerParameters
import java.util.concurrent.TimeUnit

class ReminderWorker(appContext: android.content.Context, workerParams: WorkerParameters) : Worker(appContext, workerParams) {

    override fun doWork(): Result {
        // Send notification or perform task here
        showNotification("Reminder", "Time for a reminder!")
        return Result.success()
    }
```

}

Schedule the Worker

```kotlin
val workRequest = PeriodicWorkRequestBuilder<ReminderWorker>(15, TimeUnit.MINUTES).build()
WorkManager.getInstance(this).enqueue(workRequest)
```

Example Project: Setting Up Notifications for Reminders or News Updates

Let's build a simple app that uses notifications and background services to remind the user every 15 minutes with a notification message.

Step 1: Set Up the Layout

In activity_main.xml, create a layout with a single button to start reminders.

```xml
<?xml version="1.0" encoding="utf-8"?>
<LinearLayout
xmlns:android="http://schemas.android.com/apk/res/android"
    android:layout_width="match_parent"
    android:layout_height="match_parent"
    android:orientation="vertical"
    android:gravity="center"
```

```
    android:padding="16dp">

    <Button
        android:id="@+id/startReminderButton"
        android:layout_width="wrap_content"
        android:layout_height="wrap_content"
        android:text="Start Reminders" />
</LinearLayout>
```

Step 2: Implement MainActivity

1. **Initialize the Button** to start the reminder service.
2. **Set up Notification Channel** and permissions for Android 13 and above.

```
kotlin
import android.Manifest
import android.content.pm.PackageManager
import android.os.Build
import android.os.Bundle
import android.widget.Button
import androidx.appcompat.app.AppCompatActivity
import androidx.core.app.ActivityCompat
import androidx.core.content.ContextCompat

class MainActivity : AppCompatActivity() {
```

```
  override fun onCreate(savedInstanceState: Bundle?) {
    super.onCreate(savedInstanceState)
    setContentView(R.layout.activity_main)

    createNotificationChannel()

    val startReminderButton: Button =
findViewById(R.id.startReminderButton)
    startReminderButton.setOnClickListener {
      scheduleReminder()
    }

    if (Build.VERSION.SDK_INT >=
Build.VERSION_CODES.TIRAMISU) {
      if (ContextCompat.checkSelfPermission(this,
Manifest.permission.POST_NOTIFICATIONS) !=
PackageManager.PERMISSION_GRANTED) {
        ActivityCompat.requestPermissions(this,
arrayOf(Manifest.permission.POST_NOTIFICATIONS), 1)
      }
    }
  }

  private fun createNotificationChannel() {
```

```
        // Call the createNotificationChannel() function here to set up notification channels
    }

    private fun scheduleReminder() {
        // Schedule WorkManager here for periodic reminders
    }
}
```

Step 3: Implement ReminderWorker for Background Reminders

The ReminderWorker will handle sending a notification every 15 minutes.

kotlin

Copy code

```
import android.content.Context
import androidx.work.Worker
import androidx.work.WorkerParameters

class ReminderWorker(context: Context, workerParams: WorkerParameters) : Worker(context, workerParams) {

    override fun doWork(): Result {
        showNotification("Reminder", "Time to check the app!")
        return Result.success()
```

```
    }

    private fun showNotification(title: String, message: String) {
        val channelId = "reminder_channel"
        val notificationId = 1
        val builder = NotificationCompat.Builder(applicationContext,
channelId)
            .setSmallIcon(R.drawable.ic_notification)
            .setContentTitle(title)
            .setContentText(message)
            .setPriority(NotificationCompat.PRIORITY_DEFAULT)
            .setAutoCancel(true)

NotificationManagerCompat.from(applicationContext).notify(notif
icationId, builder.build())
    }
}
```

Step 4: Schedule the Worker in MainActivity

Set up the WorkManager in scheduleReminder() to execute every 15 minutes.

kotlin

```
private fun scheduleReminder() {
```

```
val workRequest = PeriodicWorkRequestBuilder<ReminderWorker>(15, TimeUnit.MINUTES).build()
    WorkManager.getInstance(this).enqueue(workRequest)
}
```

Step 5: Run the App

1. Run the app on an emulator or physical device.
2. Tap **Start Reminders**.
3. You should receive a notification every 15 minutes, reminding you to check the app.

In this chapter, we explored how to create notifications and manage background tasks with services in Android. We learned how to set up notification channels, create and display notifications, and use WorkManager for background tasks. In the example project, we set up a periodic notification reminder to alert the user every 15 minutes, simulating a reminder or news update feature.

With these skills, you can build apps that keep users informed, even when they're not actively using the app. In the next chapter, we'll dive into advanced topics in Android development, such as Firebase integration, to add features like analytics, authentication, and real-time databases.

CHAPTER 17: HANDLING PERMISSIONS IN ANDROID

Permissions are a key part of the Android security model, providing users control over the data and features an app can access. As of Android 6.0 (API level 23), apps need to request certain permissions at runtime, giving users the ability to approve or deny requests as needed. This chapter will cover how to work with Android permissions, request and manage permissions dynamically, and build a practical example app that requests location or camera access.

Understanding Android Permissions: Overview of Runtime Permissions

Permissions are categorized into **normal permissions** and **dangerous permissions**:

1. **Normal Permissions**: These permissions have minimal risk to the user's privacy or security and are automatically granted. Examples include INTERNET and ACCESS_NETWORK_STATE.

2. **Dangerous Permissions**: These permissions give the app access to sensitive user data or functionality and must be requested at runtime. Examples include ACCESS_FINE_LOCATION, READ_CONTACTS, and CAMERA.

Permission Groups: Permissions are grouped into categories such as Location, Contacts, Camera, etc. If a user grants one permission in a group, subsequent permissions within the same group are often granted automatically.

Runtime Permission Flow:

1. Check if the permission is already granted.
2. If not, request the permission from the user.
3. Handle the user's response (granted or denied).

Requesting Permissions: How to Ask for and Manage Permissions

1. **Declare Permissions in AndroidManifest.xml**: Add the required permissions to the manifest file. For example, to access location and camera:

   xml

```
<uses-permission
android:name="android.permission.ACCESS_FINE_LOC
ATION" />
<uses-permission
android:name="android.permission.CAMERA" />
```

2. **Check for Permissions at Runtime**: Before accessing a feature, check if the app already has permission.

```kotlin
if (ContextCompat.checkSelfPermission(this,
Manifest.permission.CAMERA) ==
PackageManager.PERMISSION_GRANTED) {
    // Permission is granted, proceed with the action
} else {
    // Permission is not granted, request the permission
}
```

3. **Request Permission from the User**: If the permission is not already granted, request it using ActivityCompat.requestPermissions().

```kotlin
ActivityCompat.requestPermissions(this,
arrayOf(Manifest.permission.CAMERA),
CAMERA_PERMISSION_REQUEST_CODE)
```

4. **Handle the User's Response**: Override onRequestPermissionsResult to handle the user's response to the permission request.

kotlin

```
override fun onRequestPermissionsResult(requestCode: Int,
permissions: Array<String>, grantResults: IntArray) {
  if (requestCode ==
CAMERA_PERMISSION_REQUEST_CODE) {
    if ((grantResults.isNotEmpty() && grantResults[0] ==
PackageManager.PERMISSION_GRANTED)) {
      // Permission granted
    } else {
      // Permission denied
    }
  }
}
```

5. **Explain the Permission if Necessary**: Use shouldShowRequestPermissionRationale() to check if the user previously denied the permission and explain why it's needed.

kotlin

```
if
(ActivityCompat.shouldShowRequestPermissionRationale(
this, Manifest.permission.CAMERA)) {
   // Show explanation to the user
} else {
   // Request permission
   ActivityCompat.requestPermissions(this,
arrayOf(Manifest.permission.CAMERA),
CAMERA_PERMISSION_REQUEST_CODE)
}
```

Practical Example: An App Requiring Location and Camera Access

Let's build a simple app that requests both location and camera access. This app will check for permissions and provide feedback based on the user's response.

Step 1: Define Permissions in AndroidManifest.xml

Add the necessary permissions for location and camera access.

```
xml
<uses-permission
android:name="android.permission.ACCESS_FINE_LOCATION"
/>
<uses-permission android:name="android.permission.CAMERA"
/>
```

Step 2: Set Up the Layout in activity_main.xml

Create a layout with two buttons: one for accessing the camera and one for accessing the user's location.

```xml
xml
<?xml version="1.0" encoding="utf-8"?>
<LinearLayout
xmlns:android="http://schemas.android.com/apk/res/android"
    android:layout_width="match_parent"
    android:layout_height="match_parent"
    android:orientation="vertical"
    android:padding="16dp"
    android:gravity="center">

    <Button
        android:id="@+id/locationButton"
        android:layout_width="wrap_content"
        android:layout_height="wrap_content"
        android:text="Access Location" />

    <Button
        android:id="@+id/cameraButton"
        android:layout_width="wrap_content"
        android:layout_height="wrap_content"
        android:text="Access Camera"
        android:layout_marginTop="16dp" />
```

</LinearLayout>

Step 3: Implement Permission Handling in MainActivity

In MainActivity, implement the logic to request and handle location and camera permissions.

1. Define constants for permission request codes.

   ```kotlin
   private val LOCATION_PERMISSION_REQUEST_CODE = 100
   private val CAMERA_PERMISSION_REQUEST_CODE = 101
   ```

2. Set up the button click listeners to check and request permissions.

   ```kotlin
   import android.Manifest
   import android.content.pm.PackageManager
   import android.os.Bundle
   import android.widget.Button
   import android.widget.Toast
   import androidx.appcompat.app.AppCompatActivity
   import androidx.core.app.ActivityCompat
   import androidx.core.content.ContextCompat
   ```

```
class MainActivity : AppCompatActivity() {

  override fun onCreate(savedInstanceState: Bundle?) {
    super.onCreate(savedInstanceState)
    setContentView(R.layout.activity_main)

    val locationButton: Button = findViewById(R.id.locationButton)
    val cameraButton: Button = findViewById(R.id.cameraButton)

    locationButton.setOnClickListener {
      checkLocationPermission()
    }

    cameraButton.setOnClickListener {
      checkCameraPermission()
    }
  }

  private fun checkLocationPermission() {
    if (ContextCompat.checkSelfPermission(this, Manifest.permission.ACCESS_FINE_LOCATION) == PackageManager.PERMISSION_GRANTED) {
```

```
        // Location permission is granted
        Toast.makeText(this, "Location permission granted!", Toast.LENGTH_SHORT).show()
    } else {
        // Request location permission
        ActivityCompat.requestPermissions(this, arrayOf(Manifest.permission.ACCESS_FINE_LOCATION), LOCATION_PERMISSION_REQUEST_CODE)
    }
}

private fun checkCameraPermission() {
    if (ContextCompat.checkSelfPermission(this, Manifest.permission.CAMERA) == PackageManager.PERMISSION_GRANTED) {
        // Camera permission is granted
        Toast.makeText(this, "Camera permission granted!", Toast.LENGTH_SHORT).show()
    } else {
        // Request camera permission
        ActivityCompat.requestPermissions(this, arrayOf(Manifest.permission.CAMERA), CAMERA_PERMISSION_REQUEST_CODE)
    }
}
```

}

3. Override onRequestPermissionsResult to handle permission results.

```
kotlin
override fun onRequestPermissionsResult(requestCode: Int,
permissions: Array<String>, grantResults: IntArray) {
    super.onRequestPermissionsResult(requestCode,
permissions, grantResults)

    when (requestCode) {
        LOCATION_PERMISSION_REQUEST_CODE -> {
            if (grantResults.isNotEmpty() && grantResults[0]
== PackageManager.PERMISSION_GRANTED) {
                Toast.makeText(this, "Location permission
granted!", Toast.LENGTH_SHORT).show()
            } else {
                Toast.makeText(this, "Location permission
denied.", Toast.LENGTH_SHORT).show()
            }
        }
        CAMERA_PERMISSION_REQUEST_CODE -> {
            if (grantResults.isNotEmpty() && grantResults[0]
== PackageManager.PERMISSION_GRANTED) {
```

```
                Toast.makeText(this,    "Camera    permission
granted!", Toast.LENGTH_SHORT).show()
            } else {
                Toast.makeText(this,    "Camera    permission
denied.", Toast.LENGTH_SHORT).show()
            }
        }
    }
}
```

Step 4: Handling Permission Rationale

If the user denies a permission, provide additional context with shouldShowRequestPermissionRationale().

```kotlin
private fun showLocationRationale() {
  if
(ActivityCompat.shouldShowRequestPermissionRationale(this,
Manifest.permission.ACCESS_FINE_LOCATION)) {
    // Show an explanation to the user
    Toast.makeText(this, "Location access is required to find
nearby places.", Toast.LENGTH_LONG).show()
  }
  ActivityCompat.requestPermissions(this,
arrayOf(Manifest.permission.ACCESS_FINE_LOCATION),
LOCATION_PERMISSION_REQUEST_CODE)
```

```
}
```

Update checkLocationPermission() to call this function if needed.

kotlin

Copy code

```
if (ActivityCompat.shouldShowRequestPermissionRationale(this,
Manifest.permission.ACCESS_FINE_LOCATION)) {
  showLocationRationale()
} else {
  ActivityCompat.requestPermissions(this,
arrayOf(Manifest.permission.ACCESS_FINE_LOCATION),
LOCATION_PERMISSION_REQUEST_CODE)
}
```

In this chapter, you learned about the Android permissions model and how to handle runtime permissions. We covered the basics of normal and dangerous permissions, how to check and request permissions, and how to respond to user actions in granting or denying permissions. Finally, we built an example app that requests access to location and camera permissions, providing feedback based on the user's response.

Handling permissions is crucial for creating secure and user-friendly apps that respect user privacy. In the next chapter, we'll explore advanced Android development topics, including database integration and cloud services, to help you add even more powerful features to your applications.

CHAPTER 18: ANIMATIONS AND MOTION

Animations are a powerful way to make Android apps feel more interactive and polished. They provide visual feedback, enhance transitions, and create a smooth user experience. In this chapter, we'll cover the basics of animation in Android, explore property animations for animating views, and build a project that uses animations to improve user experience.

Basics of Animation in Android: Different Types of Animations Available

Android offers various types of animations to enhance UI components, improve transitions, and create dynamic effects. Here are the main animation types:

1. **Property Animations** (Android 3.0 and above): Allows for precise and complex animations on view properties (like translation, rotation, scaling, and alpha). The **Property**

Animator API is the most powerful animation framework in Android.

2. **View Animations**: Used for simple animations like translation, scaling, rotation, and fading. Commonly applied to UI elements like buttons or images, these animations are easy to set up but lack flexibility for complex animations.
3. **Drawable Animations**: Defined in XML for frame-by-frame animations (e.g., showing multiple images in sequence). Useful for simple animated effects like progress indicators or loading icons.
4. **MotionLayout** (Android 4.0 and above): Built on ConstraintLayout, MotionLayout provides advanced animations, interactions, and complex transitions between layout states.

Using Property Animations: Animating Views with Property Animator

The **Property Animator** API provides robust tools for creating custom animations by modifying view properties like position, size, rotation, and opacity over time. The primary classes used for property animations include ObjectAnimator, ValueAnimator, and AnimatorSet.

ObjectAnimator

ObjectAnimator allows you to animate specific properties of a view. For example, you can animate the alpha property of a view to create a fade-in effect.

```kotlin
val fadeInAnimator = ObjectAnimator.ofFloat(view, "alpha", 0f, 1f)
fadeInAnimator.duration = 1000 // Duration in milliseconds
fadeInAnimator.start()
```

In this example, the alpha property of the view animates from 0 (fully transparent) to 1 (fully opaque), creating a fade-in effect.

ValueAnimator

ValueAnimator generates values over a specified duration. You can use it to create custom animations by interpolating between values.

Example: Animating a view to move horizontally from 0 to 500 pixels.

```kotlin
val animator = ValueAnimator.ofFloat(0f, 500f)
animator.duration = 1000
animator.addUpdateListener { animation ->
   val animatedValue = animation.animatedValue as Float
   view.translationX = animatedValue
}
```

```kotlin
animator.start()
```

AnimatorSet

AnimatorSet allows you to combine multiple animations and control their sequence, either playing them together or one after another.

Example: Moving and fading a view simultaneously.

```kotlin
val moveAnimator = ObjectAnimator.ofFloat(view, "translationX", 0f, 300f)
val fadeAnimator = ObjectAnimator.ofFloat(view, "alpha", 1f, 0f)

val animatorSet = AnimatorSet()
animatorSet.playTogether(moveAnimator, fadeAnimator)
animatorSet.duration = 1000
animatorSet.start()
```

In this example, the view moves horizontally and fades out at the same time.

Common Properties to Animate

- alpha: Controls the opacity (from 0 to 1).
- translationX / translationY: Moves the view horizontally or vertically.
- scaleX / scaleY: Scales the view horizontally or vertically.
- rotation: Rotates the view in degrees.

Example Project: Adding Animations to Improve User Experience

Let's build a simple project where we add animations to enhance user interactions. We'll create an app with buttons that animate when clicked, providing visual feedback and a more engaging experience.

Step 1: Define the Layout

In activity_main.xml, create a layout with multiple buttons to apply different animations.

```xml
xml
<?xml version="1.0" encoding="utf-8"?>
<LinearLayout
xmlns:android="http://schemas.android.com/apk/res/android"
    android:layout_width="match_parent"
    android:layout_height="match_parent"
    android:orientation="vertical"
    android:padding="16dp"
    android:gravity="center">

    <Button
        android:id="@+id/fadeButton"
        android:layout_width="wrap_content"
        android:layout_height="wrap_content"
        android:text="Fade In" />
```

```
    <Button
        android:id="@+id/scaleButton"
        android:layout_width="wrap_content"
        android:layout_height="wrap_content"
        android:text="Scale Up"
        android:layout_marginTop="16dp" />

    <Button
        android:id="@+id/rotateButton"
        android:layout_width="wrap_content"
        android:layout_height="wrap_content"
        android:text="Rotate"
        android:layout_marginTop="16dp" />

    <Button
        android:id="@+id/translateButton"
        android:layout_width="wrap_content"
        android:layout_height="wrap_content"
        android:text="Move Right"
        android:layout_marginTop="16dp" />

</LinearLayout>
```

Step 2: Implement Animations in MainActivity

In MainActivity, add click listeners to each button to apply different animations using property animations.

```kotlin
import android.animation.ObjectAnimator
import android.os.Bundle
import android.widget.Button
import androidx.appcompat.app.AppCompatActivity

class MainActivity : AppCompatActivity() {

    override fun onCreate(savedInstanceState: Bundle?) {
        super.onCreate(savedInstanceState)
        setContentView(R.layout.activity_main)

        val fadeButton: Button = findViewById(R.id.fadeButton)
        val scaleButton: Button = findViewById(R.id.scaleButton)
        val rotateButton: Button = findViewById(R.id.rotateButton)
        val translateButton: Button =
findViewById(R.id.translateButton)

        fadeButton.setOnClickListener {
            fadeInAnimation(fadeButton)
        }

        scaleButton.setOnClickListener {
```

```
            scaleUpAnimation(scaleButton)
        }

        rotateButton.setOnClickListener {
            rotateAnimation(rotateButton)
        }

        translateButton.setOnClickListener {
            moveRightAnimation(translateButton)
        }
    }

    private fun fadeInAnimation(view: Button) {
        val fadeInAnimator = ObjectAnimator.ofFloat(view, "alpha",
0f, 1f)
        fadeInAnimator.duration = 1000
        fadeInAnimator.start()
    }

    private fun scaleUpAnimation(view: Button) {
        val scaleX = ObjectAnimator.ofFloat(view, "scaleX", 1f, 1.5f)
        val scaleY = ObjectAnimator.ofFloat(view, "scaleY", 1f, 1.5f)
        scaleX.duration = 500
        scaleY.duration = 500
        scaleX.start()
```

```
        scaleY.start()
    }

    private fun rotateAnimation(view: Button) {
        val rotateAnimator = ObjectAnimator.ofFloat(view, "rotation", 0f, 360f)
        rotateAnimator.duration = 1000
        rotateAnimator.start()
    }

    private fun moveRightAnimation(view: Button) {
        val translateXAnimator = ObjectAnimator.ofFloat(view, "translationX", 0f, 200f)
        translateXAnimator.duration = 1000
        translateXAnimator.start()
    }
}
```

Explanation:

- **fadeInAnimation**: The alpha property animates from 0 (transparent) to 1 (opaque), creating a fade-in effect.
- **scaleUpAnimation**: The scaleX and scaleY properties animate to increase the button's size by 1.5 times.
- **rotateAnimation**: The rotation property animates the button to rotate 360 degrees.

- **moveRightAnimation**: The translationX property animates the button to move horizontally by 200 pixels.

Step 3: Run the App

Run the app on an emulator or device and tap each button to see the animations in action. Each button should perform its respective animation, adding a lively touch to the UI.

In this chapter, you learned about Android animations and how to use the Property Animator API for creating engaging, smooth animations. We covered the basics of property animations using ObjectAnimator, ValueAnimator, and AnimatorSet to apply effects like fading, scaling, rotating, and moving views. Finally, we built a practical example app that uses these animations to enhance user interactions with buttons.

With these animation skills, you can make your apps more dynamic, intuitive, and engaging for users. In the next chapter, we'll delve into testing and debugging techniques, which are crucial for ensuring that your app works correctly and provides a positive user experience.

CHAPTER 19: FIREBASE INTEGRATION

Firebase is a powerful platform by Google that provides a suite of tools to help developers build, improve, and grow their apps. Firebase offers services like real-time databases, authentication, cloud functions, storage, and more. In this chapter, we'll cover an overview of Firebase, how to set up Firebase Authentication, and how to use the Firebase Realtime Database. We'll build a simple login system that stores user data in Firebase.

What is Firebase?

Firebase is a comprehensive platform for mobile and web app development. It offers various backend services to simplify app development, including:

1. **Firebase Authentication**: Provides a secure and easy way to manage user sign-in with email, password, phone

number, and third-party providers like Google, Facebook, and Twitter.

2. **Firebase Realtime Database**: A cloud-hosted, NoSQL database that stores and syncs data in real-time. Ideal for collaborative applications and real-time data updates.
3. **Firebase Firestore**: A flexible, scalable database similar to Realtime Database, but optimized for complex data structures.
4. **Firebase Cloud Storage**: Allows you to store user-generated content like photos, videos, and other files.
5. **Firebase Analytics**: Provides insights into user behavior and engagement.
6. **Firebase Cloud Messaging (FCM)**: Enables sending notifications to users on multiple platforms.
7. **Firebase Hosting**: Delivers web content quickly with a global CDN.

Firebase is widely used because it abstracts many backend complexities, enabling developers to focus on the core app experience.

Using Firebase Authentication: Setting Up User Authentication

Firebase Authentication provides easy-to-use and secure ways to authenticate users, supporting multiple providers (email, Google, Facebook, etc.).

Step 1: Set Up Firebase Project

1. Go to the Firebase Console and create a new project.
2. Register your Android app within the project by adding the package name and SHA-1 certificate fingerprint.
3. Download the google-services.json file and place it in the app directory of your Android project.

Step 2: Add Firebase SDK

In your build.gradle (project-level), add the Google services classpath.

```
gradle
dependencies {
  classpath 'com.google.gms:google-services:4.3.10' // Add this line
}
```

In your build.gradle (app-level), add Firebase Authentication and apply the Google services plugin.

```
gradle
plugins {
  id 'com.android.application'
  id 'com.google.gms.google-services' // Add this line
}

dependencies {
  implementation 'com.google.firebase:firebase-auth:21.0.1'
}
```

Sync the project to install dependencies.

Step 3: Implement Firebase Authentication

Firebase Authentication supports different sign-in methods. Here, we'll use email and password sign-in.

1. **Initialize FirebaseAuth** in your main activity or a dedicated authentication class.

   kotlin
   ```
   import com.google.firebase.auth.FirebaseAuth

   private lateinit var auth: FirebaseAuth

   override fun onCreate(savedInstanceState: Bundle?) {
       super.onCreate(savedInstanceState)
       setContentView(R.layout.activity_main)

       auth = FirebaseAuth.getInstance()
   }
   ```

2. **Sign Up a New User** with email and password.

   kotlin
   ```
   fun createUser(email: String, password: String) {
       auth.createUserWithEmailAndPassword(email,
   password)
   ```

```
        .addOnCompleteListener(this) { task ->
            if (task.isSuccessful) {
                // User registered successfully
                val user = auth.currentUser
                Toast.makeText(this, "User registered: ${user?.email}", Toast.LENGTH_SHORT).show()
            } else {
                // Registration failed
                Toast.makeText(this, "Registration failed: ${task.exception?.message}", Toast.LENGTH_SHORT).show()
            }
        }
}
```

3. **Sign In Existing User** with email and password.

kotlin

```
fun signInUser(email: String, password: String) {
    auth.signInWithEmailAndPassword(email, password)
        .addOnCompleteListener(this) { task ->
            if (task.isSuccessful) {
                // Sign-in successful
                val user = auth.currentUser
                Toast.makeText(this, "Welcome back: ${user?.email}", Toast.LENGTH_SHORT).show()
```

```
            } else {
                // Sign-in failed
                Toast.makeText(this, "Sign-in failed: ${task.exception?.message}", Toast.LENGTH_SHORT).show()
            }
        }
}
```

4. **Sign Out** the user.

```kotlin
fun signOutUser() {
    auth.signOut()
    Toast.makeText(this, "User signed out", Toast.LENGTH_SHORT).show()
}
```

Firebase Realtime Database: Storing and Retrieving Data in Real-Time

The Firebase Realtime Database allows data to be stored in the cloud and synchronized in real-time across clients.

Step 1: Enable Realtime Database in Firebase Console

1. In the Firebase Console, go to your project.
2. Select **Realtime Database** and click **Create Database**.

3. Set the database rules to allow read and write access (for testing only).

```json
{
  "rules": {
    ".read": "auth != null",
    ".write": "auth != null"
  }
}
```

Step 2: Add Firebase Database SDK

In your build.gradle (app-level), add the Firebase Database dependency.

```gradle
dependencies {
    implementation 'com.google.firebase:firebase-database:20.0.4'
}
```

Step 3: Create and Initialize Database References

1. **Get a Database Reference** to store user information.

```kotlin
import com.google.firebase.database.FirebaseDatabase

private val database = FirebaseDatabase.getInstance()
```

```
private val userRef = database.getReference("users")
```

2. **Save Data** to the Database.

```
kotlin
data class User(val userId: String, val email: String)

fun saveUserData(userId: String, email: String) {
  val user = User(userId, email)
  userRef.child(userId).setValue(user)
    .addOnSuccessListener {
      Toast.makeText(this, "User data saved successfully", Toast.LENGTH_SHORT).show()
    }
    .addOnFailureListener {
      Toast.makeText(this, "Failed to save user data", Toast.LENGTH_SHORT).show()
    }
}
```

3. **Retrieve Data** from the Database.

```
fun getUserData(userId: String) {
  userRef.child(userId).get()
    .addOnSuccessListener { snapshot ->
      val user = snapshot.getValue(User::class.java)
      if (user != null) {
```

```
            Toast.makeText(this, "User: ${user.email}",
Toast.LENGTH_SHORT).show()
        }
    }
    .addOnFailureListener {
        Toast.makeText(this, "Failed to retrieve user data",
Toast.LENGTH_SHORT).show()
    }
}
```

Example Project: A Simple Login System with User Data Stored in Firebase

Let's create a simple login system where users can sign up, log in, and have their data stored in the Firebase Realtime Database.

Step 1: Define the Layout

In activity_main.xml, create input fields for email and password, and buttons for login, signup, and sign-out.

```xml
<LinearLayout
xmlns:android="http://schemas.android.com/apk/res/android"
  android:layout_width="match_parent"
  android:layout_height="match_parent"
  android:orientation="vertical"
  android:padding="16dp">
```

```
<EditText
    android:id="@+id/emailEditText"
    android:layout_width="match_parent"
    android:layout_height="wrap_content"
    android:hint="Email" />

<EditText
    android:id="@+id/passwordEditText"
    android:layout_width="match_parent"
    android:layout_height="wrap_content"
    android:hint="Password"
    android:inputType="textPassword" />

<Button
    android:id="@+id/signupButton"
    android:layout_width="wrap_content"
    android:layout_height="wrap_content"
    android:text="Sign Up" />

<Button
    android:id="@+id/loginButton"
    android:layout_width="wrap_content"
    android:layout_height="wrap_content"
    android:text="Login"
    android:layout_marginTop="8dp" />
```

```
    <Button
        android:id="@+id/logoutButton"
        android:layout_width="wrap_content"
        android:layout_height="wrap_content"
        android:text="Logout"
        android:layout_marginTop="8dp" />
</LinearLayout>
```

Step 2: Implement MainActivity

In MainActivity, implement the methods for signing up, logging in, signing out, and saving user data in Firebase.

```kotlin
import android.os.Bundle
import android.widget.Button
import android.widget.EditText
import android.widget.Toast
import androidx.appcompat.app.AppCompatActivity
import com.google.firebase.auth.FirebaseAuth
import com.google.firebase.database.FirebaseDatabase

class MainActivity : AppCompatActivity() {

    private lateinit var auth: FirebaseAuth
    private val database = FirebaseDatabase.getInstance()
```

```
private val userRef = database.getReference("users")

override fun onCreate(savedInstanceState: Bundle?) {
    super.onCreate(savedInstanceState)
    setContentView(R.layout.activity_main)

    auth = FirebaseAuth.getInstance()

    val emailEditText: EditText =
findViewById(R.id.emailEditText)
    val passwordEditText: EditText =
findViewById(R.id.passwordEditText)
    val signupButton: Button = findViewById(R.id.signupButton)
    val loginButton: Button = findViewById(R.id.loginButton)
    val logoutButton: Button = findViewById(R.id.logoutButton)

    signupButton.setOnClickListener {
        val email = emailEditText.text.toString()
        val password = passwordEditText.text.toString()
        createUser(email, password)
    }

    loginButton.setOnClickListener {
        val email = emailEditText.text.toString()
        val password = passwordEditText.text.toString()
```

```
        signInUser(email, password)
      }

      logoutButton.setOnClickListener {
        signOutUser()
      }
    }

    private fun createUser(email: String, password: String) {
      auth.createUserWithEmailAndPassword(email, password)
        .addOnCompleteListener(this) { task ->
          if (task.isSuccessful) {
            val user = auth.currentUser
            if (user != null) {
              saveUserData(user.uid, email)
              Toast.makeText(this, "User registered:
${user.email}", Toast.LENGTH_SHORT).show()
            }
          } else {
            Toast.makeText(this, "Registration failed:
${task.exception?.message}", Toast.LENGTH_SHORT).show()
          }
        }
    }
```

```
private fun signInUser(email: String, password: String) {
    auth.signInWithEmailAndPassword(email, password)
        .addOnCompleteListener(this) { task ->
            if (task.isSuccessful) {
                Toast.makeText(this, "Welcome back: ${auth.currentUser?.email}", Toast.LENGTH_SHORT).show()
            } else {
                Toast.makeText(this, "Sign-in failed: ${task.exception?.message}", Toast.LENGTH_SHORT).show()
            }
        }
}

private fun signOutUser() {
    auth.signOut()
    Toast.makeText(this, "User signed out", Toast.LENGTH_SHORT).show()
}

private fun saveUserData(userId: String, email: String) {
    val user = User(userId, email)
    userRef.child(userId).setValue(user)
        .addOnSuccessListener {
            Toast.makeText(this, "User data saved successfully", Toast.LENGTH_SHORT).show()
```

```
        }
        .addOnFailureListener {
          Toast.makeText(this, "Failed to save user data",
Toast.LENGTH_SHORT).show()
        }
  }
}
```

In this code:

- **createUser()** registers a new user and saves the user data in Firebase Realtime Database.
- **signInUser()** logs in an existing user.
- **signOutUser()** logs the user out of Firebase.
- **saveUserData()** saves the user's ID and email in the Realtime Database.

In this chapter, you learned about Firebase and its core capabilities, focusing on Firebase Authentication and the Firebase Realtime Database. We covered setting up user authentication, creating user accounts, and saving user data in a real-time, cloud-hosted database. Finally, we built a practical example project with a basic login system that saves user information in Firebase.

With Firebase, you have a powerful platform that simplifies backend tasks and enables you to focus on creating engaging user experiences. In the next chapter, we'll explore integrating cloud messaging to enable push notifications, allowing you to keep users informed even when they're not actively using your app.

CHAPTER 20: TESTING AND DEBUGGING

Testing and debugging are essential steps in the app development process, helping you identify and fix issues before releasing your app to users. Testing ensures the app behaves as expected, while debugging allows you to resolve issues that arise during development. In this chapter, we'll cover the importance of testing, explore frameworks like JUnit for unit testing and Espresso for UI testing, and review effective debugging techniques using Android Studio's built-in tools.

Importance of Testing

Testing is a critical part of software development. Proper testing leads to reliable, robust, and user-friendly applications. Here are some of the main reasons testing is essential:

1. **Error Prevention**: Testing helps catch bugs and errors early, minimizing the impact on users and reducing costly fixes later in development.

2. **Improved User Experience**: Well-tested apps provide a smoother experience, increasing user satisfaction and engagement.
3. **Code Reliability and Maintainability**: Testing verifies that your code behaves as expected, making it easier to refactor and maintain over time.
4. **Faster Development**: Automated tests allow for quick validation of new code, leading to faster, more efficient development cycles.

Unit Testing and UI Testing: Introduction to Testing Frameworks like JUnit and Espresso

Android supports various types of testing, but two of the most commonly used are unit testing and UI testing.

1. Unit Testing with JUnit

Unit testing focuses on testing individual components of your app, such as functions or classes, to ensure they perform as expected. JUnit is the most widely used testing framework for unit tests in Android.

Setting Up JUnit Tests:

1. **Add JUnit Dependency**: Most Android projects come with JUnit by default, but ensure it's in your build.gradle file (app-level).

```
gradle
dependencies {
    testImplementation 'junit:junit:4.13.2'
}
```

2. **Create a Unit Test Class**: Inside the src/test/java directory, create a new class for your tests.

```
kotlin
import org.junit.Assert.assertEquals
import org.junit.Test

class CalculatorTest {

    @Test
    fun addition_isCorrect() {
        val result = Calculator.add(2, 3)
        assertEquals(5, result)
    }
}
```

3. **Run the Test**: Right-click the test file or method and select **Run** to execute the test. The test should pass if the expected output matches the actual result.

Common Assertions in JUnit:

- assertEquals(expected, actual): Checks if two values are equal.
- assertTrue(condition): Checks if the condition is true.
- assertFalse(condition): Checks if the condition is false.
- assertNull(object): Checks if the object is null.

JUnit tests are quick to execute and provide immediate feedback, making them ideal for testing app logic, algorithms, and utility functions.

2. UI Testing with Espresso

UI Testing (or integration testing) checks if the app's user interface behaves correctly, ensuring that interactions like button clicks, text input, and navigation work as expected. Espresso is a popular Android framework for UI testing.

Setting Up Espresso Tests:

1. **Add Espresso Dependencies**:

```
gradle
dependencies {
    androidTestImplementation
'androidx.test.espresso:espresso-core:3.4.0'
    androidTestImplementation 'androidx.test.ext:junit:1.1.3'
}
```

2. **Create an Espresso Test Class**: In the src/androidTest/java directory, create a new class for UI tests.

```
kotlin
import androidx.test.ext.junit.runners.AndroidJUnit4
import androidx.test.rule.ActivityTestRule
import org.junit.Rule
import org.junit.Test
import org.junit.runner.RunWith

import androidx.test.espresso.Espresso.onView
import androidx.test.espresso.action.ViewActions.click
import androidx.test.espresso.action.ViewActions.typeText
import
androidx.test.espresso.matcher.ViewMatchers.withId
import
androidx.test.espresso.matcher.ViewMatchers.withText

@RunWith(AndroidJUnit4::class)
class LoginActivityTest {

  @Rule @JvmField
  val activityRule =
ActivityTestRule(LoginActivity::class.java)
```

```
    @Test
    fun testLoginButton_clickable() {

onView(withId(R.id.usernameEditText)).perform(typeText
("user"))

onView(withId(R.id.passwordEditText)).perform(typeText
("password"))
        onView(withId(R.id.loginButton)).perform(click())

        onView(withText("Login
Successful")).check(matches(isDisplayed()))
    }
}
```

3. **Run the Test**: Right-click the test file or method and select **Run** to execute the test on an emulator or device. Espresso simulates user actions and validates if the UI responds as expected.

Common Espresso Actions:

- click(): Simulates a click on a view.
- typeText(string): Types text into a text input field.
- closeSoftKeyboard(): Closes the on-screen keyboard.
- matches(matcher): Checks if a view matches certain criteria.

UI tests ensure that your app's user interface functions correctly, providing confidence that the app delivers a consistent user experience.

Debugging Tips: Common Debugging Practices and Using the Android Studio Debugger

Debugging is the process of identifying, analyzing, and fixing issues in your code. Android Studio provides powerful tools for debugging, making it easier to resolve problems quickly.

Using the Android Studio Debugger

The Android Studio debugger offers several features to help you track down issues:

1. **Setting Breakpoints**: Breakpoints pause the app at specific lines of code, allowing you to inspect variables and the program's state.
   - Click on the left margin next to the line number to add a breakpoint.
   - Run your app in **Debug** mode (green bug icon) to trigger breakpoints during execution.
2. **Step Through Code**: Use the following commands to move through your code line-by-line:
   - **Step Over** (F8): Executes the current line and moves to the next line.

  - **Step Into** (F7): Steps into a method to debug it.
  - **Step Out** (Shift+F8): Completes the current method and returns to the calling code.

3. **Inspect Variables**: When the code pauses at a breakpoint, you can inspect the values of variables in the **Variables** pane. This view shows local variables, their current values, and data types.
4. **Evaluate Expressions**: The **Evaluate Expression** window lets you check the results of expressions without modifying your code. This is useful for testing calculations, inspecting objects, or calling functions during a debugging session.
5. **Using Logcat**: Logcat displays system messages, app logs, and error messages, providing valuable insights during development and debugging.
   - **Logging Messages**: Use Log.d, Log.i, Log.e, etc., to output custom messages.

     ```kotlin
     Log.d("MainActivity", "App has started")
     ```

   - **Logcat Filters**: Filter logs by tag, priority, or keyword to focus on specific information.

Debugging Tips and Best Practices:

1. **Use Logging**: Use Log.d, Log.i, and other logging methods to print information about the app's state, such as variable values and method execution points.
2. **Test Edge Cases**: Identify and test unusual cases, like empty inputs, large datasets, and error scenarios.
3. **Binary Search for Bugs**: If you encounter unexpected behavior, use breakpoints and log statements to narrow down the problematic code by testing half of the code each time.
4. **Analyze Stack Traces**: When your app crashes, Android Studio provides a stack trace showing the sequence of function calls that led to the crash. Review the stack trace to pinpoint where the error occurred.
5. **Use Assertions**: Add assertions to verify assumptions in your code and catch issues early. For example, assert(value != null) ensures a variable isn't null at a specific point in your code.

Practical Example: Testing and Debugging a Simple Calculator

Let's apply these testing and debugging techniques with a simple calculator app that includes unit tests and UI tests. This app will have a method to add two numbers and a button to trigger the calculation.

Step 1: Create the Calculator Class

In the main package, create a class with an add method.

```kotlin
object Calculator {
    fun add(a: Int, b: Int): Int {
        return a + b
    }
}
```

Step 2: Write a Unit Test for the Calculator

1. Create a test class for the Calculator in the src/test/java directory.
2. Add test methods for different input scenarios.

```kotlin
import org.junit.Assert.assertEquals
import org.junit.Test

class CalculatorTest {

    @Test
    fun addition_isCorrect() {
        assertEquals(5, Calculator.add(2, 3))
        assertEquals(0, Calculator.add(-3, 3))
        assertEquals(-5, Calculator.add(-2, -3))
    }
}
```

Step 3: Write a UI Test for Calculator Button

Suppose our app has a button that calculates the sum of two numbers and displays the result.

1. Create a UI test class in the src/androidTest/java directory.
2. Add a test to simulate entering numbers and pressing the button.

kotlin

Copy code

```
import androidx.test.ext.junit.runners.AndroidJUnit4
import androidx.test.rule.ActivityTestRule
import org.junit.Rule
import org.junit.Test
import org.junit.runner.RunWith
import androidx.test.espresso.Espresso.onView
import androidx.test.espresso.action.ViewActions.click
import androidx.test.espresso.action.ViewActions.typeText
import androidx.test.espresso.matcher.ViewMatchers.withId
import androidx.test.espresso.matcher.ViewMatchers.withText
import androidx.test.espresso.assertion.ViewAssertions.matches

@RunWith(AndroidJUnit4::class)
class CalculatorActivityTest {

  @Rule @JvmField
```

```
  val activityRule =
ActivityTestRule(CalculatorActivity::class.java)

  @Test
  fun testAddition() {
    onView(withId(R.id.num1EditText)).perform(typeText("2"))
    onView(withId(R.id.num2EditText)).perform(typeText("3"))
    onView(withId(R.id.calculateButton)).perform(click())

onView(withId(R.id.resultTextView)).check(matches(withText("5
")))
  }
}
```

Step 4: Debug the Application

Run the tests and use the debugging tools if any test fails or the app behaves unexpectedly. Set breakpoints and inspect variables to understand why certain tests might fail or where issues arise in the code.

In this chapter, we covered the importance of testing and debugging in Android development. We explored unit testing with JUnit and UI testing with Espresso, enabling us to verify both the logic and UI of our app. Additionally, we discussed effective debugging techniques using Android Studio's tools, such as breakpoints, variable inspection, and Logcat.

Testing and debugging are crucial steps that contribute to creating reliable, user-friendly, and well-maintained applications. In the next chapter, we'll dive into advanced topics like performance optimization, which will help ensure your app runs smoothly and efficiently, even on lower-end devices.

CHAPTER 21: APP OPTIMIZATION AND PERFORMANCE

Optimizing your app's performance is critical for providing a smooth user experience, reducing battery usage, and ensuring efficient memory management. In this chapter, we'll explore tips for improving performance by managing memory, battery, and responsiveness. We'll also cover network optimization techniques, such as caching and background loading, and discuss practical tips for identifying and fixing common performance issues.

Improving Performance: Tips on Managing Memory, Battery Usage, and Responsiveness

Optimizing an app's performance involves several aspects: managing memory effectively, reducing battery drain, and ensuring smooth UI responsiveness.

1. Managing Memory

Efficient memory usage is crucial for preventing slowdowns, freezes, or crashes. Here are some techniques to optimize memory usage:

- **Avoid Memory Leaks**: A memory leak happens when an object is unintentionally retained in memory even after it's no longer needed. To prevent memory leaks:
  - Use weak references where possible.
  - Release resources, listeners, or services in onDestroy() or onPause() methods.
  - Avoid storing references to Activity or Context in static variables.
  - Use **LeakCanary**, a memory leak detection library, to identify and resolve memory leaks during development.
- **Use Efficient Data Structures**: Choose data structures wisely. For example, use SparseArray instead of HashMap when mapping integers to objects, as it's optimized for memory efficiency.
- **Optimize Bitmap Usage**: Loading large images can consume significant memory, leading to **OutOfMemoryError**. To avoid this:
  - Downscale images to fit the view.
  - Use BitmapFactory.Options to load images in a reduced resolution.

- Use caching libraries like **Glide** or **Picasso** for efficient image loading and caching.

2. Reducing Battery Usage

Battery efficiency is vital for mobile applications, especially those running in the background or using hardware-intensive resources like GPS. Here are some battery-saving tips:

- **Optimize Location Services**:
  - Use coarse location instead of fine location if precise GPS data isn't necessary.
  - Request location updates only when needed and stop updates when the user isn't interacting with location-based features.
  - Use **Geofencing** or **Activity Recognition** API to reduce continuous GPS use for location tracking.
- **Minimize Background Processing**:
  - Avoid background tasks that aren't necessary, and schedule periodic tasks with **WorkManager** instead of Service to benefit from optimized battery scheduling.
  - Use **JobScheduler** or **AlarmManager** to perform background tasks based on conditions, like network connectivity or device charging status.
- **Reduce Wake Lock Usage**: Wake locks prevent the device from sleeping, which drains battery. Use wake locks

sparingly and release them as soon as they're no longer needed.

3. Ensuring UI Responsiveness

A smooth user experience relies on consistent UI responsiveness. To keep the UI responsive:

- **Avoid Blocking the Main Thread**: The main UI thread handles rendering, user input, and more. Avoid lengthy operations (like network requests, file I/O, or complex calculations) on the main thread.
    - Use **AsyncTask**, **HandlerThread**, or **Coroutines** for background processing.
    - Use **RecyclerView** instead of ListView for better scrolling performance on lists.
- **Reduce Overdraw**: Overdraw occurs when the app draws pixels multiple times on the screen. Use the **Show GPU Overdraw** option in **Developer Options** to check and reduce overdraw by simplifying layouts and reducing overlapping views.

Optimizing Network Calls: Using Caching, Background Loading, and Efficient APIs

Network calls are often a source of slowdowns and battery drain. Optimizing network usage can significantly improve an app's performance.

1. Caching Data

Caching helps reduce redundant network requests, saving bandwidth and speeding up data retrieval. Consider these caching strategies:

- **Use HTTP Caching**: Many REST APIs support HTTP caching through headers like ETag and Cache-Control. Use a caching library like **OkHttp** to handle HTTP caching automatically.

  kotlin

  ```
  val cacheSize = (10 * 1024 * 1024).toLong() // 10 MB
  val cache = Cache(cacheDir, cacheSize)

  val okHttpClient = OkHttpClient.Builder()
      .cache(cache)
      .build()
  ```

- **Database Caching**: For apps with frequently accessed data, consider saving data locally in a database (like Room) and syncing updates from the server periodically. This reduces the need for constant network requests.
- **Image Caching**: For apps that display many images, use an image caching library like **Glide** or **Picasso**. These libraries cache images locally, reducing redundant image downloads.

2. Background Loading

Loading data in the background enhances performance and responsiveness:

- **Load Data in Background Threads**: Use AsyncTask, Executors, or Kotlin Coroutines to handle data loading outside the main thread, preventing UI freezes.
- **Lazy Loading for Lists**: For long lists, implement lazy loading by fetching data incrementally as the user scrolls. Libraries like **Paging 3** simplify pagination by loading data in chunks and caching previous items.

3. Optimize API Calls

Efficient API usage reduces data load and improves app performance:

- **Optimize JSON Responses**: If you control the API, minimize response payload by sending only the required data. Remove unnecessary fields and use lightweight formats like JSON.
- **Batch API Requests**: Reduce the number of network requests by batching multiple operations into a single request if the API supports it.
- **Use WebSockets for Real-Time Data**: For real-time applications, such as chat or live updates, consider using WebSockets instead of HTTP polling. WebSockets

maintain a persistent connection, reducing repeated requests.

Practical Optimization Tips: Identifying and Fixing Common Performance Issues in Apps

Here are practical tips and tools to help you identify and fix performance bottlenecks:

1. Use Android Profiler for Performance Analysis

Android Studio's **Profiler** provides insights into CPU, memory, network, and battery usage, helping you locate performance issues.

- **CPU Profiler**: Identifies CPU-intensive tasks and excessive method calls. Use it to detect bottlenecks, especially on the main thread.
- **Memory Profiler**: Tracks memory usage and detects memory leaks. It visualizes memory allocation, helping you identify potential leaks and excessive memory usage.
- **Network Profiler**: Monitors network requests, their sizes, and response times. Use it to identify slow or excessive network calls.
- **Energy Profiler**: Monitors battery usage, especially for background tasks, GPS, and other power-intensive features.

2. Reduce Layout Complexity

Complex layouts can slow down rendering and affect performance. Follow these tips:

- **Flatten Layouts**: Avoid deeply nested layouts by using ConstraintLayout, which reduces hierarchy levels and improves rendering speed.
- **Use ViewStub**: ViewStub is an invisible, lightweight placeholder that only loads when you need it, reducing initial layout inflation time.
- **Use RecyclerView for Lists**: RecyclerView is optimized for large data sets, reusing item views to improve scrolling performance and memory usage.

3. Optimize Bitmap and Image Handling

Large bitmaps can consume significant memory and processing power, slowing down the app:

- **Resize Images**: Scale down images to match the display size. For example, if an image is displayed in a 100x100 ImageView, load it at that resolution rather than its original size.
- **Use Vector Drawables**: For simple icons and shapes, use vector drawables instead of bitmap images, as they scale without consuming extra memory.

4. Reduce Start-Up Time

Slow app startup times can lead to a poor user experience. To optimize startup:

- **Defer Initialization**: Initialize only essential components on startup, and delay non-critical processes until later.
- **Optimize Cold Starts**: Avoid heavy operations, like network requests, during app launch. Use splash screens only if they serve a purpose (such as loading essential data).
- **Use Lazy Initialization**: Only create objects when they're needed, rather than during app startup.

5. Optimize Database Queries

Efficient database queries help prevent UI lags:

- **Use Indexes**: Index frequently queried columns to speed up query performance in SQLite or Room databases.
- **Reduce Query Frequency**: Cache data from the database in memory if it's frequently accessed, reducing redundant database queries.
- **Use Projections**: Query only the fields needed, rather than fetching entire objects.

Example Optimization Project: Improving an Image-Loading App

Let's apply some of these optimization techniques to an image-loading app that fetches and displays images from a server.

Step 1: Set Up Image Loading with Glide

Glide is an optimized library for handling images, including caching and resizing.

kotlin

```
import com.bumptech.glide.Glide

val imageView: ImageView = findViewById(R.id.imageView)
Glide.with(this)
    .load("https://example.com/image.jpg")
    .placeholder(R.drawable.placeholder)
    .error(R.drawable.error_image)
    .into(imageView)
```

This code handles caching and resizing automatically, reducing memory usage and download frequency.

Step 2: Lazy Load Images in a RecyclerView

When displaying a list of images, use RecyclerView with lazy loading for smooth scrolling. Glide's caching will optimize image retrieval, preventing redundant downloads.

kotlin

```
class ImageAdapter(private val imageUrls: List<String>) :
RecyclerView.Adapter<ImageAdapter.ImageViewHolder>() {

    class ImageViewHolder(view: View) :
RecyclerView.ViewHolder(view) {
        val imageView: ImageView =
view.findViewById(R.id.imageView)
    }
```

```
    override fun onCreateViewHolder(parent: ViewGroup, viewType: Int): ImageViewHolder {
        val view = LayoutInflater.from(parent.context).inflate(R.layout.item_image, parent, false)
        return ImageViewHolder(view)
    }

    override fun onBindViewHolder(holder: ImageViewHolder, position: Int) {
        val url = imageUrls[position]
        Glide.with(holder.imageView.context)
            .load(url)
            .into(holder.imageView)
    }

    override fun getItemCount(): Int = imageUrls.size
}
```

Step 3: Optimize Network Calls with OkHttp Caching

Use OkHttp's caching to avoid redundant network calls when reloading the same images.

kotlin

```
val cacheSize = (10 * 1024 * 1024).toLong() // 10 MB
```

```
val cache = Cache(cacheDir, cacheSize)

val okHttpClient = OkHttpClient.Builder()
    .cache(cache)
    .build()
```

Configure Glide to use this OkHttp client, enabling cached images to load quickly even without a network connection.

In this chapter, we explored essential performance optimization techniques for Android applications, including memory management, battery efficiency, and UI responsiveness. We covered network optimization strategies like caching and lazy loading and discussed practical tips for identifying and fixing common performance issues using tools like Android Profiler.

By following these optimization practices, you can create Android apps that provide a smooth, responsive user experience while conserving resources and ensuring efficient operation on various devices. In the next chapter, we'll look at preparing your app for release, including testing, security, and publishing best practices.

CHAPTER 22: PUBLISHING YOUR APP ON GOOGLE PLAY STORE

Publishing an app on the Google Play Store opens it up to millions of potential users worldwide. This chapter will guide you through preparing your app for release, creating a Google Play Developer Account, navigating the publishing process, and finally, marketing and maintaining your app for long-term success.

Preparing for Launch: Steps to Prepare Your App for Release

Before publishing your app, ensure it is polished, optimized, and thoroughly tested. Here are key steps to prepare your app for a successful launch:

1. **Finalize UI and Features**: Ensure your app's UI is consistent, easy to use, and aligned with Android design guidelines. All features should be functional and tested on various devices.

2. **Testing and Debugging**:
   - **Device Testing**: Test on multiple devices, screen sizes, and Android versions to identify and resolve compatibility issues.
   - **Testing Types**: Conduct unit testing (JUnit), UI testing (Espresso), and performance testing (Android Profiler).
   - **Beta Testing**: Use Google Play's beta testing feature or platforms like Firebase App Distribution to gather user feedback before launch.
3. **Optimize for Performance**:
   - **Memory and CPU Usage**: Use Android Profiler to optimize memory and CPU usage.
   - **App Size**: Reduce your app's size by removing unused resources, minifying code, and using ProGuard or R8 for code shrinking and obfuscation.
4. **Prepare for Different Configurations**:
   - **Localization**: Translate text and support multiple languages if you plan to release internationally.
   - **Permissions and Privacy**: Ensure permissions are only requested when needed, and comply with Google's privacy policy for handling user data.
5. **Build and Sign the Release APK**:
   - **Generate a Signed APK**: In Android Studio, go to **Build > Generate Signed Bundle/APK** to create a

release APK or Android App Bundle (AAB). AAB is preferred for publishing on the Play Store as it optimizes app size for different devices.

- **Secure Keystore**: Use a secure, private keystore file to sign your app. Back up your keystore, as it is required for future updates.

Creating a Developer Account: Setting Up a Google Play Developer Account

To publish on the Play Store, you'll need a Google Play Developer Account. Here's how to set it up:

1. **Go to the Google Play Console**: Visit Google Play Console and sign in with your Google account.
2. **Pay the Developer Registration Fee**: A one-time registration fee of $25 is required. This gives you lifetime access to the Play Console and the ability to publish apps.
3. **Complete the Registration Form**:
    - Fill out necessary information, including your developer name, email, and other contact details.
    - Agree to Google Play's developer policies and guidelines.
4. **Set Up Payment Profile** (Optional): If your app includes in-app purchases, set up a Google payments profile to

receive revenue. You can do this in **Payments > Settings** within the Google Play Console.

Publishing Process: Uploading Your APK, Adding Descriptions, and Setting Up Pricing

Once your developer account is ready, follow these steps to publish your app on the Google Play Store:

Step 1: Create a New App in the Play Console

1. In the Play Console, click **Create App** and provide the following details:
    - **App Name**: The name users will see on the Play Store.
    - **Default Language**: The primary language for your app listing.
    - **App or Game**: Specify whether your app is an application or a game.
    - **Free or Paid**: Decide if your app will be free or paid (this cannot be changed after publishing).
2. Click **Create** to continue.

Step 2: Complete App Details

In the **App Content** section, you'll need to provide detailed information about your app:

- **App Details**:

  - **Title**: The app's name (limit: 50 characters).
  - **Short Description**: A brief description that appears in search results (limit: 80 characters).
  - **Full Description**: A detailed description of your app's features, benefits, and purpose (limit: 4000 characters). Include keywords that help your app appear in searches.
- **Graphic Assets**:
  - **App Icon**: 512x512 pixels in PNG format.
  - **Feature Graphic**: 1024x500 pixels, used as the main visual on your app's Play Store listing.
  - **Screenshots**: Minimum of 2, but up to 8 screenshots per supported device type (e.g., phone, tablet). Show essential screens and highlight key features.
- **Video (Optional)**: Include a YouTube video URL that showcases your app, such as a tutorial or promotional video.

Step 3: Set Up Pricing and Distribution

In the **Pricing & Distribution** section:

1. **Select Countries**: Choose the countries or regions where you want to make the app available.
2. **Set Up Pricing**: If your app is paid, set a price and review Google's revenue-sharing terms. Paid apps also require a Google payments profile.

3. **Target Audience and Content Rating**:
   - Specify your app's target audience (e.g., children, teens, adults).
   - Complete the **Content Rating Questionnaire** to receive a rating (e.g., Everyone, Teen) that appears on your app listing.
4. **App Category**: Choose the appropriate category (e.g., Education, Health, Productivity).

Step 4: Upload Your App Bundle (AAB)

In the **Release > Production** section:

1. **Create a New Release**: Click **Create New Release** to start a new release.
2. **Upload Your App Bundle (AAB)**:
   - Click **Upload** and select your signed AAB file. Google recommends using AAB over APK as it optimizes the download size for users.
3. **Add Release Notes**: Describe the changes in this version (e.g., new features, bug fixes). Users will see this information in the update details.
4. **Review and Release**: Once all details are completed, review your submission and click **Rollout to Production** to publish the app.

Step 5: App Review and Approval

After you submit your app, Google will review it to ensure it complies with Play Store policies. Reviews typically take a few hours to a couple of days, depending on the app's complexity and Google's review workload.

Marketing and Maintenance Tips: How to Promote Your App and Maintain It with Updates

Once your app is live, marketing and maintenance are key to long-term success. Here are some tips:

1. Marketing Your App

- **Social Media and Online Presence**: Promote your app on social media platforms, create a website or landing page, and use blogs to reach your target audience.
- **App Store Optimization (ASO)**: Optimize your app listing with relevant keywords, engaging descriptions, and high-quality screenshots. Encourage users to leave positive reviews, as higher ratings improve visibility.
- **Influencer Partnerships**: Collaborate with influencers or bloggers in your app's niche to reach a broader audience.
- **Run Ad Campaigns**: Use Google Ads or social media ads to promote your app, targeting audiences based on location, interests, and demographics.

- **Email Marketing**: Build an email list or send notifications to keep users engaged and informed about updates, new features, or promotions.

2. Maintaining and Updating Your App

- **Monitor Performance and User Feedback**: Regularly check the **Google Play Console** for app analytics, crash reports, and user feedback to understand your app's performance and areas of improvement.
- **Release Regular Updates**: Regular updates keep users engaged and show that you're actively maintaining the app. Updates can include:
    - New features or improvements.
    - Bug fixes to address reported issues.
    - Performance enhancements based on usage data.
- **Implement User Feedback**: Listen to user feedback to understand their needs and make improvements. Prompt responses to user reviews can also enhance your app's reputation.
- **Test New Features in Stages**: Google Play Console allows you to use staged rollouts to release updates gradually. This way, you can monitor the update's performance on a subset of users before releasing it to everyone.
- **Adhere to Play Store Policies**: Stay up-to-date with Google Play's policies and guidelines. Violations can result

in suspension, so regularly review updates to the policies, especially regarding user data, security, and in-app purchases.

In this chapter, you learned how to publish an Android app on the Google Play Store, covering everything from preparing the app for release to setting up a Google Play Developer Account. We went through the steps to upload your APK or AAB, fill out your app listing, and submit it for review. Additionally, we explored strategies for marketing your app to increase visibility and tips for maintaining and updating it to ensure continued success.

Publishing on the Google Play Store opens up opportunities for global reach and user engagement. With thoughtful marketing and consistent updates, you can maximize your app's impact and user satisfaction. Congratulations on reaching this milestone in your app development journey!

www.ingramcontent.com/pod-product-compliance
Lightning Source LLC
LaVergne TN
LVHW051440050326
832903LV00030BD/3188

* 9 7 9 8 3 4 5 5 6 0 0 2 0 *